Contemporary Challenges: Navigating the Complex World of Politics and Social Sciences

Laurel D. Malvern

Copyright and Legal Disclaimer

This book is a work of nonfiction. The names, characters, organizations, places, events, and incidents mentioned herein are either the products of the author's research or used in a factual manner. Any resemblance to actual persons, living or dead, or actual events is purely coincidental.

The author has made every effort to ensure the accuracy and completeness of the information contained in this book. However, the author and publisher assume no responsibility for errors, omissions, inaccuracies, or any inconsistency herein. The information provided is on an "as is" basis and without warranties of any kind, either express or implied. The reader assumes all responsibility for the use of this information and shall waive any claims of liability or damages against the author or publisher.

The views and opinions expressed in this book are those of the author and do not necessarily reflect the official policy or position of any organization or entity mentioned. Any advice or strategies contained herein may not be suitable for every situation. Readers are advised to consult with professionals where appropriate.

"Contemporary Challenges: Navigating the Complex World
of Politics and Social Sciences"

Preface 8

Chapter 1: Overview of the Current Landscape in Politics and Social Sciences 12

Chapter 2: The Importance of Understanding Interconnected Issues 15

Chapter 3: Climate Change and Environmental Policy 19

Chapter 4: Overview of Global Warming and Its Scientific Basis 23

Chapter 5: Key Environmental Policies and International Agreements 27

Chapter 6: Role of Activism in Driving Change 31

Chapter 7: Case Studies: Successful Sustainability Initiatives 36

Chapter 8: Racial Justice and Inequality 40

Chapter 9: Historical Context of Systemic Racism 44

Chapter 10: Diversity and Inclusion Efforts in Various Sectors 48

Chapter 11: Case Studies: Impactful Racial Justice Campaigns 51

Chapter 12: Immigration and Border Issues: Historical Trends in Immigration Policies 54

Chapter 13: Current Refugee Crises and Humanitarian Responses: Analysis of Border Control Policies 57

Chapter 14: Case Studies: Stories from the Frontlines 60

Chapter 15: Political Polarization: Causes of Political Division in Modern Societies 62

Chapter 16: Impact of Polarization on Governance and Society: Strategies for Bridging the Divide 65

Chapter 17: Case Studies: Efforts to Reduce Polarization 68

Chapter 18: Globalization: Impacts and Challenges 71

Chapter 19: Definition and History of Globalization: Economic, Political, and Cultural Impacts 74

Chapter 20: Benefits and Challenges of Globalization 78

Chapter 21: Case Studies: Globalization's Effects on Local Communities 81

Chapter 22: Economic Inequality: Causes, Consequences, and Solutions 84

Chapter 23: Examination of Wealth Disparity and its Roots: Impact of Economic Policies on Poverty 87

Chapter 24: Proposals for Economic Reforms: Towards a More Just and Inclusive Economy 90

Chapter 25: Case Studies: Successful Initiatives to Reduce Inequality 93

Chapter 26: Gender Studies: Understanding Gender Equality and Equity 96

Chapter 27: History and Evolution of Feminism: Current Issues in Gender Identity and LGBTQ+ Rights 99

Chapter 28: Intersectionality and Its Significance: Case Studies of Prominent Gender Rights Movements 102

Chapter 29: Populism and Nationalism: Global Trends and Case Studies 105

Chapter 30: Healthcare Policy: Systems, Debates, and Case Studies 108

Chapter 31: Criminal Justice Reform: Systems, Calls, and Case Studies 111

Chapter 32: Media and Fake News: Influence, Issues, and Case Studies 114

Chapter 33: Cybersecurity and Data Privacy: Threats, Importance, and Case Studies 117

Chapter 34: International Relations: Strategies, Conflicts, and Diplomacy 120

Chapter 35: Election Integrity and Voting Rights: Challenges, Security, and Case Studies 123

Chapter 36: Mental Health in Society: Intersection, Impact, and Initiatives 126

Chapter 37: Education Policy: Systems, Equality, and Reforms 129

Chapter 38: Urban Development and Housing: Challenges, Gentrification, and Solutions 132

Chapter 39: Civil Liberties and Human Rights: Freedom, Challenges, and Victories 135

Chapter 40: Technology and Society: Impacts, Ethics, and Innovations 138

Chapter 41: Drug Policy and Substance Abuse: Laws, Treatment, and Reform 141

Chapter 42: Case Studies: Effective Substance Abuse Programs 144

Conclusion: 147

The interconnectedness of politics and social issues is undeniable, as each profoundly influences the other in a continuous cycle of impact and response. Here's how this interconnectedness manifests: 149

As we delve into the intricate web of politics and social issues, it becomes abundantly clear that change is not a passive process but an active endeavor that requires the collective efforts of individuals like you. Here's a call to action to inspire readers to engage and contribute to positive change: 151

Below is a glossary of key terms used throughout the book: 154

Preface

As I sat down to write "Contemporary Challenges: Navigating the Complex World of Politics and Social Sciences," I found myself reflecting on the myriad issues that define our times. The early 21st century is a period marked by profound change, unprecedented challenges, and remarkable opportunities. From the sweeping impacts of globalization and technological innovation to the urgent calls for social justice and environmental sustainability, we are living in an era where understanding the interconnectedness of these issues is not just beneficial but essential.

My journey in creating this book began with a simple yet powerful realization: the issues we face today are deeply intertwined, influencing and shaping one another in complex ways. This interdependence demands a holistic approach to understanding and addressing these challenges. With this in mind, I set out to explore and document the most pressing topics within the realms of politics and social sciences, aiming to provide a comprehensive and accessible guide for readers.

In writing this book, I was guided by several key objectives. First and foremost, I wanted to create a resource that would inform and empower readers. Whether you are a student seeking to deepen your knowledge, a professional navigating the complexities of your field, or an engaged citizen striving to make sense of the world, my hope is that this book will serve as a valuable tool in your journey.

Each chapter of this book delves into a specific issue, providing a thorough analysis of its history, current state, and future implications. Through extensive research and compelling case studies, I have endeavored to present a balanced and nuanced perspective on each topic. From the escalating crisis of climate change to the persistent struggle for racial justice, from the contentious debates over immigration to the polarizing effects of political partisanship, every chapter is designed to shed light on the critical challenges of our time.

One of the most rewarding aspects of writing this book has been the opportunity to highlight the voices and stories of individuals and communities who are at the forefront of these issues. Their experiences, struggles, and triumphs offer invaluable insights and inspiration. It is through their stories that we can gain a deeper understanding of the human dimension of these challenges and the profound impact they have on our lives.

As you read through the pages of "Contemporary Challenges,"
I encourage you to approach each topic with an open mind
and a critical eye. Consider how these issues intersect and
what they mean for you personally, your community, and the
world at large. Engage with the questions raised and reflect on
the solutions proposed. It is my hope that this book will not
only inform you but also inspire you to take action, to
contribute to the ongoing conversations and efforts to address
these pressing issues.

In closing, I want to express my gratitude to the many
individuals who have contributed to this book. To the
scholars, activists, policymakers, and everyday citizens whose
insights and experiences have enriched these pages, thank you
for your invaluable contributions. I also extend my deepest
appreciation to my readers — your curiosity, passion, and
commitment to understanding and addressing the challenges
of our time are the driving forces behind this work.

We are at a pivotal moment in history. The choices we make
and the actions we take today will shape the future for
generations to come. Let us navigate these contemporary
challenges with wisdom, compassion, and a steadfast
commitment to creating a better, more just world.

Sincerely,

Laurel D. Malvern

Chapter 1: Overview of the Current Landscape in Politics and Social Sciences

Introduction
The early 21st century is characterized by rapid change and complexity. Politics and social sciences are fields that not only document these changes but also seek to understand and address them. This chapter provides an overview of the current landscape, highlighting the interconnected nature of political, social, and economic issues that define our times.

Political Dynamics
The political landscape today is marked by significant polarization and division. Ideological battles, both within and between nations, are shaping governance and public policy. Key trends include:

Rise of Populism: Populist movements have gained traction globally, challenging traditional political structures and elites.

Nationalism vs. Globalism: A tension exists between nationalist movements advocating for sovereign interests and globalist perspectives promoting international cooperation.
Impact of Social Media: Digital platforms play a crucial role in political communication, often amplifying polarized viewpoints and misinformation.
Social Issues
Social sciences help us understand the profound shifts occurring in societies around the world. Key social issues include:

Racial Justice: Movements like Black Lives Matter highlight ongoing struggles against systemic racism and inequality.
Gender Equality: The fight for gender rights and LGBTQ+ inclusion continues to gain momentum, challenging traditional norms and seeking legal reforms.
Economic Disparities: Economic inequality is a pervasive issue, with wealth gaps widening both within and between countries.
Environmental Concerns
Environmental policy has become a central issue in both politics and social sciences due to the pressing threat of climate change. Key points include:

Climate Change: Global warming and its impacts are driving policy changes and environmental activism.
Sustainability: There is a growing emphasis on sustainable practices in business, governance, and daily life to combat environmental degradation.
International Agreements: Agreements like the Paris Climate Accord aim to coordinate global efforts to address climate challenges.
Technological Advancements
Technological progress is reshaping society in unprecedented ways. Key areas of focus include:

Cybersecurity: As our reliance on digital infrastructure grows, so too does the importance of protecting data and privacy.
Artificial Intelligence: AI and automation are transforming industries, raising questions about employment and ethical considerations.
Digital Divide: Access to technology remains unequal, with significant disparities in digital literacy and infrastructure across different regions.
Economic Trends
The global economy is undergoing significant shifts influenced by various political and social factors. Key trends include:

Globalization: While globalization has brought economic growth, it has also led to cultural homogenization and economic disparities.
Trade Policies: Trade wars and protectionist policies are impacting international relations and economic stability.
Economic Reforms: Discussions on wealth distribution, taxation, and social safety nets are at the forefront of economic policy debates.
Health and Wellbeing
Public health issues have come to the forefront, particularly in light of recent global health crises. Key considerations include:

Healthcare Systems: Debates on healthcare accessibility, affordability, and quality continue to shape policy.
Mental Health: There is increasing recognition of the importance of mental health and the need for comprehensive mental health policies.
Global Health Initiatives: International cooperation is crucial in addressing pandemics and other global health challenges.
Conclusion

The current landscape in politics and social sciences is dynamic and multifaceted. Understanding the interplay between political actions, social movements, environmental concerns, technological advancements, economic trends, and health issues is essential for navigating the complexities of our world. This chapter sets the stage for deeper explorations of these themes in the subsequent chapters, providing readers with the context needed to engage with the pressing issues of our time.

Chapter 2: The Importance of Understanding Interconnected Issues

Introduction
In an increasingly complex world, the interconnections between political, social, economic, and environmental issues are more apparent than ever. Understanding these interconnected issues is crucial for devising effective solutions and creating meaningful change. This chapter explores why it is essential to recognize and analyze the interrelated nature of contemporary challenges and how this approach can lead to more comprehensive and sustainable solutions.

The Web of Interconnected Issues
*1. The Complexity of Modern Challenges

Modern issues are rarely isolated. They are part of a larger, interconnected web where actions in one area can have significant ripple effects in others.
Examples include how economic policies affect social inequality, or how environmental degradation impacts public health.
**2. Globalization's Role

Globalization has intensified these connections, making it clear that local issues often have global repercussions and vice versa.
Economic decisions made in one country can influence employment, environmental policies, and social stability in another.
Case Studies of Interconnected Issues
**1. Climate Change and Social Inequality

Climate change disproportionately affects marginalized communities, exacerbating existing social inequalities.
Policies aimed at reducing carbon emissions must also consider social justice to ensure equitable outcomes.
**2. Health Crises and Economic Stability

The COVID-19 pandemic illustrated how health crises can disrupt global economies, highlighting the need for robust public health systems to maintain economic stability.
Economic measures taken to address the pandemic's impact, such as stimulus packages, also affect long-term fiscal health and social welfare.
**3. Technological Advancements and Privacy

The rise of digital technology brings benefits but also raises concerns about data privacy and security.

Balancing innovation with the protection of individual rights requires integrated policy approaches that address both technological progress and ethical considerations.
Benefits of Understanding Interconnected Issues
**1. Holistic Policy Making

Policies that recognize interconnectedness are more likely to address root causes rather than just symptoms.
Holistic approaches can lead to more effective and sustainable solutions by considering the broader impact of decisions.
**2. Enhanced Problem-Solving

Understanding the relationships between issues enables more comprehensive problem-solving strategies.
Stakeholders from different sectors can collaborate more effectively when they see the links between their areas of focus.
**3. Informed Public Discourse

Public awareness of interconnected issues fosters more informed and engaged citizens.
Educated discourse can lead to greater public support for integrated and multifaceted policies.
Strategies for Addressing Interconnected Issues
**1. Interdisciplinary Research and Collaboration

Encouraging collaboration across academic disciplines can provide deeper insights into the connections between issues.
Interdisciplinary research helps build a more nuanced understanding of complex problems.
**2. Integrated Policy Frameworks

Developing policy frameworks that explicitly address the interplay between various issues can lead to more coherent and effective governance.

Examples include environmental policies that also promote social equity and economic growth.
**3. Community Engagement and Participation

Engaging communities in the policy-making process ensures that diverse perspectives are considered.
Participation from all societal sectors can help identify interconnected issues and develop more inclusive solutions.
**4. Education and Awareness

Promoting education that emphasizes the interconnectedness of global issues can prepare future leaders to tackle these challenges.
Awareness campaigns can highlight how individual actions contribute to broader societal impacts.
Conclusion
Understanding the interconnected nature of contemporary challenges is essential for crafting effective solutions and fostering sustainable development. Recognizing these connections enables policymakers, researchers, and citizens to approach problems holistically, considering the wide-ranging impacts of their actions. As we move forward, embracing the complexity and interdependence of political, social, economic, and environmental issues will be crucial in addressing the multifaceted challenges of our time.

Chapter 3: Climate Change and Environmental Policy

Introduction
Climate change is one of the most urgent and pervasive issues facing our world today. Its impacts are felt globally, influencing ecosystems, economies, and communities. Environmental policy, therefore, plays a critical role in mitigating the effects of climate change and promoting sustainable development. This chapter delves into the science behind climate change, the policies aimed at combating it, and the role of environmental activism in driving change.

The Science of Climate Change
*1. Understanding Global Warming

Global warming refers to the long-term increase in Earth's average surface temperature due to human activities, primarily the emission of greenhouse gases (GHGs) like carbon dioxide (CO2) and methane (CH4).

The greenhouse effect: GHGs trap heat in the atmosphere, leading to a warming effect.

**2. Evidence and Impact

Rising global temperatures: Average global temperatures have increased by approximately 1.2 degrees Celsius since pre-industrial times.

Melting polar ice and rising sea levels: Ice caps and glaciers are melting, contributing to sea-level rise.

Extreme weather events: Increased frequency and severity of storms, droughts, and heatwaves.

Impact on biodiversity: Species are facing habitat loss and shifting ecological niches.

**3. Scientific Consensus

The vast majority of climate scientists agree that climate change is real, primarily human-induced, and poses significant risks.

Key reports: Intergovernmental Panel on Climate Change (IPCC) assessments provide comprehensive reviews of climate science and projections.

Key Environmental Policies

*1. International Agreements

Paris Agreement (2015): A landmark accord within the United Nations Framework Convention on Climate Change (UNFCCC) aimed at limiting global warming to well below 2 degrees Celsius above pre-industrial levels, with efforts to limit the increase to 1.5 degrees.

Kyoto Protocol (1997): An earlier agreement that set binding targets for industrialized countries to reduce GHG emissions.

**2. National Policies

United States: Clean Air Act, Environmental Protection Agency (EPA) regulations, and recent initiatives like the Green New Deal proposal.
European Union: European Green Deal, which aims to make Europe climate-neutral by 2050.
China: National Action Plan on Climate Change, with significant investments in renewable energy and carbon trading schemes.
**3. Local and Regional Initiatives

Urban planning for sustainability: Cities like Copenhagen and San Francisco implementing green infrastructure and sustainable transport.
Community-based initiatives: Local projects aimed at reducing carbon footprints and promoting resilience.
The Role of Environmental Activism
*1. Grassroots Movements

Movements like Fridays for Future, led by youth activists like Greta Thunberg, have brought significant attention to the climate crisis.
Indigenous activism: Indigenous communities often lead in advocating for environmental protection, emphasizing the interconnectedness of land, culture, and climate.
**2. Non-Governmental Organizations (NGOs)

Organizations like Greenpeace, the Sierra Club, and the World Wildlife Fund (WWF) play crucial roles in advocacy, education, and direct action.
**3. Public Awareness and Education

Campaigns and educational programs aim to increase public understanding of climate issues and inspire action.
Media and arts: Documentaries, films, and art installations raising awareness and sparking conversations.

Case Studies of Successful Environmental Policies
**1. Renewable Energy Adoption

Germany's Energiewende (Energy Transition): A
comprehensive policy framework aimed at increasing
renewable energy use, enhancing energy efficiency, and
phasing out nuclear power.
Costa Rica: A leader in renewable energy, achieving nearly
100% of its electricity from renewable sources.
**2. Conservation Efforts

Amazon Rainforest: Brazil's efforts in reducing deforestation
rates through stricter enforcement and satellite monitoring.
Marine Protected Areas (MPAs): Policies to protect ocean
ecosystems, such as Australia's Great Barrier Reef Marine
Park.
**3. Sustainable Agriculture

Agroecology practices: Implementing sustainable farming
methods that enhance biodiversity, soil health, and resilience
to climate impacts.
Challenges and Future Directions
**1. Policy Implementation and Enforcement

Challenges in translating international agreements into
actionable national policies.
Issues of compliance and enforcement, particularly in
countries with limited resources.
**2. Economic and Political Barriers

The influence of powerful fossil fuel industries and economic
interests that resist change.
Political polarization and differing priorities among nations.
**3. Innovations and Opportunities

Technological advancements: Innovations in renewable energy, carbon capture, and storage technologies.
Green economy: Economic opportunities arising from sustainable practices and industries.
Conclusion
Climate change and environmental policy are deeply interconnected with virtually every aspect of modern life. Addressing this global crisis requires a multifaceted approach that includes international cooperation, national initiatives, local actions, and widespread public engagement. By understanding the science, supporting effective policies, and engaging in activism, we can collectively work towards a more sustainable and resilient future. This chapter sets the stage for exploring the broader impacts and intersections of climate change with other critical issues discussed in subsequent chapters.

Chapter 4: Overview of Global Warming and Its Scientific Basis

Introduction
Global warming, driven primarily by human activities, is a defining environmental challenge of our time. This chapter provides a comprehensive overview of the scientific basis behind global warming, examining the causes, mechanisms, and consequences of this phenomenon. Understanding the science is essential for informing effective policies and individual actions aimed at mitigating climate change and its impacts.

The Greenhouse Effect

*1. Fundamental Principles

The greenhouse effect is a natural phenomenon whereby certain gases in Earth's atmosphere trap heat from the sun, leading to a warming of the planet's surface.
Greenhouse gases (GHGs) include carbon dioxide (CO2), methane (CH4), nitrous oxide (N2O), and fluorinated gases.
**2. Enhanced Greenhouse Effect

Human activities, such as burning fossil fuels, deforestation, and industrial processes, have significantly increased the concentration of GHGs in the atmosphere.
This enhanced greenhouse effect intensifies the trapping of heat, leading to global warming.
Evidence of Global Warming
*1. Temperature Trends

Scientific data collected over decades consistently show a warming trend in global temperatures.
Surface temperature records, satellite observations, and measurements from weather stations confirm this trend.
**2. Changes in Climate Indicators

Rising sea levels: Thermal expansion and melting ice contribute to sea level rise, threatening coastal communities.
Glacier retreat: Glaciers worldwide are shrinking, leading to reduced freshwater supplies and increased risks of glacial lake outburst floods.
Shifts in precipitation patterns: Changes in rainfall and snowfall patterns affect water availability, agriculture, and ecosystems.
Attribution of Global Warming
*1. Human Influence

The Intergovernmental Panel on Climate Change (IPCC) and numerous scientific studies have concluded that human activities are the primary drivers of recent global warming. The burning of fossil fuels for energy production, transportation, and industrial processes is the largest contributor to CO_2 emissions.

**2. Natural Variability

While natural factors like volcanic eruptions and solar radiation fluctuations can influence climate, their impact on recent warming is minimal compared to human activities.

Climate Models and Projections

**1. Climate Modeling

Climate models use mathematical equations to simulate Earth's climate system, incorporating factors like atmospheric composition, ocean currents, and land surface characteristics. These models have successfully reproduced past climate variations and are used to make future projections.

**2. Projections for the Future

IPCC assessments provide a range of scenarios for future climate change based on different emission trajectories. Projections include continued warming, sea level rise, changes in precipitation patterns, and increased frequency of extreme weather events.

Consequences of Global Warming

*1. Environmental Impacts

Loss of biodiversity: Habitat loss, species extinctions, and shifts in ecosystems threaten global biodiversity.

Ocean acidification: Increased CO_2 levels lead to acidification of seawater, posing risks to marine life and coral reefs.

Amplified weather extremes: Heatwaves, droughts, hurricanes, and heavy rainfall events become more frequent and intense.

**2. Socio-Economic Effects

Disruption of agriculture: Changes in temperature and precipitation patterns affect crop yields, food security, and rural livelihoods.
Health risks: Heat-related illnesses, vector-borne diseases, and air pollution exacerbate public health challenges.
Economic costs: Damage to infrastructure, property, and natural resources result in significant economic losses.
Mitigation and Adaptation Strategies
*1. Mitigation Measures

Mitigation aims to reduce GHG emissions and limit the extent of future climate change.
Strategies include transitioning to renewable energy, improving energy efficiency, and implementing carbon pricing mechanisms.
**2. Adaptation Strategies

Adaptation involves adjusting to the impacts of climate change to minimize risks and maximize resilience.
Examples include building sea walls to protect coastal areas, implementing drought-resistant agricultural practices, and enhancing early warning systems for extreme weather events.
Conclusion
Global warming is a scientifically well-established phenomenon with far-reaching implications for the environment, society, and economy. By understanding the scientific basis behind global warming, we can appreciate the urgency of taking action to reduce emissions, mitigate impacts, and build resilience to climate change. This chapter lays the groundwork for exploring the policy responses and societal challenges associated with addressing global warming in subsequent chapters.

Chapter 5: Key Environmental Policies and International Agreements

Introduction

In response to the pressing threat of climate change and environmental degradation, nations around the world have forged international agreements and implemented environmental policies to address these challenges. This chapter examines some of the most significant environmental policies and international agreements aimed at promoting sustainability, reducing greenhouse gas emissions, and protecting ecosystems on a global scale.

The Paris Agreement
*1. Overview

The Paris Agreement, adopted in 2015 under the United Nations Framework Convention on Climate Change (UNFCCC), represents a landmark international accord on climate action.
Its central aim is to limit global warming to well below 2 degrees Celsius above pre-industrial levels, with efforts to limit the increase to 1.5 degrees.
**2. Key Provisions

Nationally Determined Contributions (NDCs): Each participating country sets its own targets for reducing greenhouse gas emissions and enhancing climate resilience.
Transparency and Accountability: Mechanisms for monitoring, reporting, and verifying countries' progress towards their goals.
Global Stocktake: Periodic assessments to review collective progress and strengthen ambition over time.
The Kyoto Protocol
*1. Historical Context

The Kyoto Protocol, adopted in 1997, was the first international agreement to set binding targets for reducing greenhouse gas emissions.

It established legally binding commitments for industrialized countries to reduce emissions by specified amounts over the period 2008-2012.
**2. Achievements and Limitations

Successes: The Kyoto Protocol catalyzed international efforts to address climate change and laid the groundwork for subsequent agreements.
Limitations: Its effectiveness was limited by the lack of participation from major emitters like the United States and the absence of binding commitments for developing countries.
National Environmental Policies
**1. United States

Clean Air Act: A comprehensive law that regulates air emissions and sets standards for air quality.
Environmental Protection Agency (EPA): The EPA plays a central role in implementing and enforcing environmental regulations, including those related to climate change.
**2. European Union

European Green Deal: A flagship initiative that aims to make the EU climate-neutral by 2050, with measures to cut greenhouse gas emissions, promote clean energy, and protect biodiversity.
**3. China

National Action Plan on Climate Change: China's strategy for addressing climate change includes targets for reducing carbon intensity, increasing renewable energy capacity, and improving energy efficiency.
Local and Regional Initiatives
*1. Urban Planning for Sustainability

Green Infrastructure: Cities like Copenhagen and Singapore invest in green spaces, public transportation, and renewable energy to promote sustainability and resilience.
Compact Development: Dense, mixed-use development patterns reduce reliance on cars and minimize urban sprawl, thus lowering carbon emissions.
**2. Community-Based Projects

Renewable Energy Cooperatives: Community-led initiatives to develop and operate renewable energy projects, such as wind farms and solar installations.
Sustainable Agriculture Programs: Local initiatives promote regenerative farming practices, organic agriculture, and community-supported agriculture (CSA) models.
Challenges and Opportunities
**1. Challenges

Political Resistance: Opposition from vested interests, lobbying efforts, and political polarization can hinder the adoption of ambitious environmental policies.
Implementation Gaps: Despite international agreements and national policies, translating commitments into concrete actions remains a challenge for many countries.
**2. Opportunities

Technological Innovations: Advances in renewable energy, energy storage, and carbon capture and storage (CCS) technologies offer promising solutions for reducing emissions.
Public Awareness and Engagement: Increasing awareness of environmental issues and fostering public participation can drive demand for policy action and accountability.
Conclusion

Environmental policies and international agreements play a crucial role in addressing climate change, protecting ecosystems, and promoting sustainable development. While significant progress has been made, the global community faces ongoing challenges in implementing and strengthening these measures. By continuing to prioritize cooperation, innovation, and public engagement, nations can work together to build a more sustainable and resilient future for generations to come. This chapter highlights the importance of collective action and the need for continued commitment to environmental stewardship at all levels of society.

Chapter 6: Role of Activism in Driving Change

Introduction
Activism has long been a powerful force for social and environmental change, mobilizing individuals and communities to advocate for justice, equality, and sustainability. This chapter explores the diverse forms of activism and their impact on shaping policies, challenging injustices, and driving positive transformations in society and the environment.

Types of Activism
*1. Grassroots Movements

Grassroots activism originates from the community level, driven by ordinary citizens organizing around shared concerns.
Examples include community organizing, protest movements, and local campaigns for environmental justice.
**2. Youth Activism

Youth activists play a prominent role in advocating for environmental sustainability, social justice, and political reform.
Movements like Fridays for Future, led by young activists such as Greta Thunberg, have gained global attention and spurred action on climate change.
**3. Online Activism

Digital platforms and social media enable online activism, allowing individuals to connect, organize, and raise awareness about various issues.

Hashtags, online petitions, and social media campaigns amplify voices and mobilize support for causes.

Environmental Activism

*1. Direct Action

Direct action tactics, such as protests, blockades, and civil disobedience, are used to raise awareness, disrupt harmful activities, and pressure decision-makers.
Examples include tree-sitting to prevent deforestation and occupying fossil fuel infrastructure to protest new pipelines.

**2. Advocacy and Policy Influence

Environmental activists engage in advocacy efforts to influence policy decisions, shape legislation, and hold governments and corporations accountable for their environmental impact.
Lobbying, litigation, and public campaigns are common strategies used to advance environmental agendas.

**3. Community-Based Conservation

Indigenous communities and local conservation groups often lead efforts to protect natural habitats, promote sustainable land management, and preserve traditional ecological knowledge.
Collaborative partnerships between communities, NGOs, and governments can enhance conservation outcomes and support local livelihoods.

Social Justice Activism

*1. Racial Justice Movements

Movements like Black Lives Matter (BLM) advocate for racial equality, police reform, and systemic change to address racism and discrimination.
Intersectional approaches recognize the interconnectedness of social justice issues, including race, gender, class, and environmental justice.

**2. Feminist Activism

Feminist activists work to challenge gender inequality, promote women's rights, and combat gender-based violence and discrimination.
Intersectional feminism emphasizes the intersection of gender with other forms of oppression and advocates for inclusive and equitable solutions.
**3. LGBTQ+ Rights Advocacy

LGBTQ+ activists advocate for equal rights, nondiscrimination protections, and societal acceptance for lesbian, gay, bisexual, transgender, and queer individuals. Pride events, awareness campaigns, and legal advocacy efforts contribute to advancing LGBTQ+ rights and visibility.
Impact and Effectiveness
*1. Policy Change

Activist movements have catalyzed policy reforms, legislative changes, and institutional improvements across a range of issues.
Examples include the civil rights movement's role in advancing voting rights and anti-discrimination laws and the environmental movement's influence on conservation policies and pollution regulations.
**2. Cultural Shifts

Activism can drive cultural shifts by challenging norms, raising consciousness, and fostering public dialogue on pressing issues.
Movements like #MeToo have sparked conversations about sexual harassment and gender-based violence, leading to increased awareness and calls for accountability.
**3. Inspiring Collective Action

Activist movements inspire individuals to get involved, join collective efforts, and contribute to positive change in their communities and beyond.
The ripple effect of activism can mobilize broader support, build solidarity networks, and sustain momentum for social and environmental justice causes.
Challenges and Strategies
**1. Repression and Backlash

Activists often face repression, intimidation, and violence from authorities, corporations, and hostile groups opposed to their agendas.
Strategies for protecting activists include legal support, solidarity networks, and international advocacy campaigns to raise awareness of human rights abuses.
**2. Maintaining Momentum

Sustaining long-term engagement and momentum is a challenge for activist movements, particularly amid shifting political climates and competing priorities.
Strategies include coalition-building, strategic planning, and fostering leadership succession to ensure continuity and resilience.
**3. Intersectionality and Solidarity

Recognizing the interconnectedness of social and environmental issues and building solidarity across movements can enhance collective power and effectiveness.
Intersectional approaches that center marginalized voices and address overlapping oppressions are essential for creating inclusive and equitable movements.
Conclusion

Activism serves as a catalyst for change, challenging power structures, amplifying marginalized voices, and advocating for a more just and sustainable world. By engaging in diverse forms of activism and working collaboratively across social and environmental movements, individuals and communities can drive meaningful progress towards addressing systemic injustices, protecting the planet, and promoting human rights. This chapter celebrates the transformative potential of activism and emphasizes the importance of collective action in shaping a better future for all.

Chapter 7: Case Studies: Successful Sustainability Initiatives

Introduction
Amid growing concerns about environmental degradation and climate change, innovative sustainability initiatives are demonstrating how businesses, governments, and communities can work together to achieve lasting environmental and social benefits. This chapter examines several case studies of successful sustainability initiatives from around the world, highlighting their strategies, impacts, and lessons learned.

1. Costa Rica's Pioneering Approach to Conservation
Overview

Background: Costa Rica is renowned for its rich biodiversity and commitment to conservation.
Initiative: The country's Payment for Environmental Services (PES) program incentivizes landowners to preserve forests and restore ecosystems by compensating them for the ecosystem services their land provides, such as carbon sequestration, watershed protection, and biodiversity conservation.
Impact: The PES program has contributed to significant increases in forest cover, protected watersheds, and biodiversity habitats, while also supporting rural livelihoods and ecotourism opportunities.
2. Denmark's Transition to Renewable Energy
Overview

Background: Denmark has emerged as a global leader in renewable energy adoption, particularly wind power.
Initiative: The Danish government's ambitious renewable energy targets, combined with supportive policies and investments in research and infrastructure, have facilitated the rapid expansion of wind energy generation.
Impact: Wind power now accounts for over 40% of Denmark's electricity consumption, reducing reliance on fossil fuels, lowering greenhouse gas emissions, and creating thousands of green jobs in the process.
3. The City of Curitiba's Sustainable Urban Development
Overview

Background: Curitiba, Brazil, is renowned for its innovative urban planning and sustainable transportation systems.
Initiative: The city's Bus Rapid Transit (BRT) system, integrated land-use planning, and extensive green spaces have transformed Curitiba into a model of sustainable urban development.
Impact: The BRT system has reduced traffic congestion, air pollution, and carbon emissions, while also promoting social inclusion, economic development, and quality of life for residents.
4. The Circular Economy Model in Amsterdam
Overview

Background: Amsterdam is pioneering the transition to a circular economy, where resources are used more efficiently and waste is minimized.
Initiative: The city's circular economy strategy focuses on initiatives such as waste-to-energy plants, sustainable procurement practices, and circular business models that prioritize product reuse, remanufacturing, and recycling.

Impact: Amsterdam's circular economy initiatives are reducing waste generation, conserving natural resources, and stimulating innovation and economic growth in sectors like green technology and sustainable design.

5. The Solar Energy Revolution in India

Overview

Background: India is rapidly expanding its solar energy capacity to meet growing energy demands while reducing reliance on fossil fuels.

Initiative: The Indian government's ambitious solar energy targets, combined with supportive policies, incentives, and investments in solar infrastructure, have facilitated the rapid deployment of solar power projects across the country.

Impact: India has become one of the world's fastest-growing solar markets, with solar energy contributing significantly to electricity generation, reducing greenhouse gas emissions, and increasing energy access in rural areas.

6. The Regenerative Agriculture Movement in California

Overview

Background: California's agriculture sector is embracing regenerative farming practices that prioritize soil health, biodiversity, and carbon sequestration.

Initiative: Farmers and ranchers are implementing techniques such as cover cropping, crop rotation, and rotational grazing to restore degraded soils, enhance ecosystem resilience, and sequester carbon in the soil.

Impact: Regenerative agriculture practices are improving soil fertility, water retention, and crop yields, while also mitigating climate change by storing carbon in the soil and reducing greenhouse gas emissions from agriculture.

Conclusion

These case studies illustrate the power of innovative sustainability initiatives to address pressing environmental and social challenges while also delivering economic benefits and enhancing quality of life. By learning from successful examples like Costa Rica's conservation program, Denmark's renewable energy transition, and Curitiba's sustainable urban planning, stakeholders around the world can emulate best practices, scale up solutions, and accelerate progress towards a more sustainable and resilient future for all.

Chapter 8: Racial Justice and Inequality

Introduction
Racial justice and inequality remain pressing issues worldwide, deeply entrenched in historical, social, and economic structures. This chapter delves into the complexities of racial injustice, exploring systemic racism, social disparities, and efforts towards achieving equity and equality for marginalized communities.

Understanding Systemic Racism
*1. Historical Context

Systemic racism refers to the pervasive and institutionalized discrimination against racial and ethnic minorities, rooted in historical patterns of oppression and exploitation.
Historical injustices such as slavery, colonialism, and segregation continue to shape contemporary racial dynamics and disparities.
**2. Structural Inequities

Systemic racism manifests in various forms, including disparities in education, employment, housing, healthcare, and criminal justice.
Structural inequities perpetuate racial disparities and limit opportunities for marginalized communities to thrive.
Social Justice Movements
*1. Civil Rights Movement

The Civil Rights Movement of the 1950s and 1960s was a watershed moment in the fight for racial equality, challenging segregation and discriminatory laws.

Key figures like Martin Luther King Jr., Rosa Parks, and
Malcolm X led nonviolent protests and advocacy efforts to
dismantle institutional racism.
**2. Black Lives Matter

The Black Lives Matter (BLM) movement emerged in response
to police violence and systemic racism against Black
communities.
BLM advocates for policy reforms, police accountability, and
an end to racial profiling and violence against people of color.
Intersectionality and Inclusive Activism
*1. Intersectional Approach

Intersectionality recognizes that individuals experience
multiple forms of oppression and discrimination based on
intersecting identities such as race, gender, class, sexuality,
and disability.
An intersectional approach to activism acknowledges the
complexities of marginalization and centers the experiences of
those most impacted by intersecting oppressions.
**2. Inclusive Activism

Inclusive activism strives to amplify marginalized voices,
challenge systemic injustices, and build solidarity across
diverse communities.
Intersectional coalitions and allyship efforts strengthen
collective resistance to racism, sexism, homophobia,
transphobia, and other forms of oppression.
Addressing Structural Inequities
*1. Policy Reforms

Policy interventions are essential for addressing systemic
racism and promoting racial equity.

Reforms may include criminal justice reform, anti-discrimination laws, affirmative action, and investments in education, healthcare, and housing in marginalized communities.
**2. Community Empowerment

Community-led initiatives empower marginalized groups to advocate for their rights, address local needs, and build collective power.
Grassroots organizations, mutual aid networks, and community centers provide spaces for organizing, education, and mutual support.
Economic Justice and Reparations
**1. Reparations

Reparations seek to address historical injustices by providing compensation, restitution, and acknowledgment to communities harmed by slavery, colonialism, and other forms of state-sanctioned violence.
Reparations can take various forms, including financial compensation, land redistribution, educational opportunities, and community development initiatives.
**2. Economic Empowerment

Economic justice initiatives aim to dismantle systemic barriers to economic opportunity and wealth accumulation for marginalized communities.
Programs such as minority business development, wealth redistribution, and job training initiatives promote economic empowerment and address racial disparities in income and wealth.
Conclusion

Racial justice and inequality are complex and multifaceted issues that require systemic solutions and collective action. By confronting systemic racism, advocating for policy reforms, and centering the voices and experiences of marginalized communities, we can work towards a more just and equitable society for all. This chapter underscores the importance of ongoing efforts to address racial injustice and build inclusive communities where everyone can thrive, regardless of race, ethnicity, or background.

Chapter 9: Historical Context of Systemic Racism

Introduction
Understanding the historical roots of systemic racism is crucial for grasping its enduring impact on society today. This chapter delves into the historical context of systemic racism, tracing its origins from colonialism and slavery to segregation and ongoing racial disparities.

Colonialism and Slavery
*1. Colonial Exploitation

European colonial powers engaged in systematic exploitation and subjugation of indigenous peoples and African populations, laying the foundation for racial hierarchies and inequality.
The transatlantic slave trade forcibly transported millions of Africans to the Americas, where they endured brutal enslavement and exploitation for centuries.
**2. Legalized Racism

Racist ideologies were used to justify the enslavement of Africans and the dispossession of indigenous lands, codifying racial hierarchies into law.
Legal frameworks such as the slave codes and Jim Crow laws enforced racial segregation, restricted rights, and perpetuated white supremacy.
Civil Rights Movement
*1. Struggle for Equality

The Civil Rights Movement of the 1950s and 1960s challenged racial segregation and discrimination, demanding equal rights and justice for African Americans.
Nonviolent protests, legal challenges, and grassroots organizing efforts led to landmark civil rights legislation, including the Civil Rights Act of 1964 and the Voting Rights Act of 1965.
**2. Legacy of Resistance

The Civil Rights Movement inspired a legacy of resistance and activism against systemic racism, paving the way for subsequent social justice movements.
Figures like Martin Luther King Jr., Rosa Parks, and Malcolm X became symbols of courage and resilience in the fight for racial equality.
Segregation and Urban Displacement
*1. Segregation

The legacy of segregation persists in many aspects of American society, including housing, education, employment, and criminal justice.
Redlining, discriminatory lending practices, and racially restrictive covenants have perpetuated residential segregation and wealth disparities between white and minority communities.
**2. Urban Displacement

Urban renewal projects, gentrification, and displacement have disproportionately affected communities of color, leading to the loss of affordable housing, cultural displacement, and economic marginalization.
Racially motivated policies and practices have contributed to the concentration of poverty and social isolation in many urban areas.
Current Social Justice Movements
*1. Black Lives Matter

The Black Lives Matter (BLM) movement emerged in response to police violence and systemic racism against Black communities.
BLM advocates for police reform, racial justice, and an end to systemic oppression and violence against people of color.
**2. Intersectional Activism

Intersectional approaches to activism recognize the interconnectedness of race, gender, class, and other social identities, highlighting the unique experiences of marginalized groups.
Movements like Say Her Name and #MeToo center the experiences of Black women and other marginalized genders in the fight against racism, sexism, and violence.
Analysis of Social Justice Movements
*1. Impact and Achievements

Social justice movements have raised awareness, mobilized communities, and pressured institutions to address systemic racism and inequality.
Policy reforms, cultural shifts, and increased accountability have been among the achievements of these movements.
**2. Challenges and Resistance

Social justice movements face opposition from entrenched power structures, including political leaders, law enforcement agencies, and white supremacist groups.
Challenges include backlash, co-optation, and efforts to discredit and undermine the legitimacy of activist movements.
Conclusion

The historical context of systemic racism provides vital insights into the enduring legacies of oppression and resistance that shape contemporary social justice movements. By understanding the roots of racial inequality and the struggles for justice that have preceded us, we can better appreciate the urgency of ongoing efforts to dismantle systemic racism and build a more equitable and inclusive society for future generations. This chapter underscores the importance of historical consciousness in informing activism and advocacy for racial justice and social change.

Chapter 10: Diversity and Inclusion Efforts in Various Sectors

Introduction
Diversity and inclusion are increasingly recognized as essential components of a thriving and equitable society. This chapter explores efforts to promote diversity and inclusion across various sectors, including business, education, government, and the arts.

Diversity in the Workplace
*1. Corporate Initiatives

Many companies have implemented diversity and inclusion initiatives to foster a more inclusive workplace culture and increase representation of underrepresented groups. Strategies may include diversity training, mentorship programs, affinity groups, and diverse hiring practices.
**2. Benefits of Diversity

Research shows that diverse teams are more innovative, productive, and better equipped to meet the needs of diverse customers and clients.
Inclusive workplaces also promote employee engagement, satisfaction, and retention.
Diversity in Education
**1. Higher Education

Colleges and universities are increasingly prioritizing diversity and inclusion in admissions, curriculum development, and student support services.

Affirmative action policies, diversity scholarships, and multicultural education programs aim to promote access and equity in higher education.
**2. K-12 Education

K-12 schools are implementing diversity and anti-bias education programs to foster inclusive learning environments and combat prejudice and discrimination.
Culturally responsive teaching practices and diverse literature help students see themselves reflected in the curriculum and promote empathy and understanding.
Diversity in Government and Public Service
*1. Representation

Efforts to increase diversity in government aim to ensure that decision-making bodies reflect the demographics of the population they serve.
Diversity initiatives may include targeted recruitment efforts, diversity training for public officials, and support for underrepresented candidates.
**2. Policy Impacts

Diverse representation in government can lead to more responsive and inclusive policymaking that addresses the needs and concerns of all communities.
Policies promoting equity, social justice, and cultural competency are more likely to be enacted and effectively implemented with diverse voices at the table.
Diversity in the Arts and Media
*1. Representation in Media

The arts and media industries play a powerful role in shaping cultural narratives and perceptions of diversity.
Efforts to increase diversity in casting, storytelling, and behind-the-scenes roles aim to create more inclusive and authentic representations of diverse experiences.

**2. Community Engagement

Arts organizations and media outlets are engaging with diverse communities to co-create content, amplify marginalized voices, and foster dialogue on important social issues.
Collaborative projects, cultural festivals, and community-led initiatives promote cultural exchange, understanding, and appreciation.
Challenges and Opportunities
*1. Persistent Inequities

Despite progress, systemic barriers to diversity and inclusion persist in many sectors, including systemic racism, sexism, ableism, and other forms of discrimination.
Addressing these challenges requires sustained commitment, systemic change, and intersectional approaches that center marginalized voices and experiences.
**2. Intersectionality and Equity

Intersectional approaches to diversity and inclusion recognize the interconnectedness of social identities and experiences, emphasizing the need for holistic and equitable solutions.
Prioritizing equity involves addressing structural inequities, redistributing power and resources, and dismantling systems of oppression that perpetuate inequality.
Conclusion
Diversity and inclusion efforts across various sectors are essential for building more equitable, inclusive, and resilient communities. By embracing diversity, challenging biases, and fostering inclusive practices, organizations and institutions can create environments where all individuals feel valued, respected, and empowered to succeed. This chapter highlights the importance of ongoing efforts to promote diversity and inclusion in pursuit of social justice and collective well-being.

Chapter 11: Case Studies: Impactful Racial Justice Campaigns

Introduction
Racial justice campaigns have played a pivotal role in raising awareness, mobilizing communities, and driving meaningful change in society. This chapter examines several case studies of impactful racial justice campaigns, highlighting their strategies, successes, and lasting legacies.

1. The Civil Rights Movement
Overview

Context: The Civil Rights Movement of the 1950s and 1960s was a watershed moment in the fight for racial equality in the United States.
Campaigns: From the Montgomery Bus Boycott to the March on Washington, civil rights activists organized nonviolent protests, legal challenges, and grassroots movements to challenge segregation and discrimination.
Impact: The Civil Rights Movement led to landmark legislation, including the Civil Rights Act of 1964 and the Voting Rights Act of 1965, which outlawed racial discrimination and secured voting rights for African Americans.
2. Black Lives Matter
Overview

Context: The Black Lives Matter (BLM) movement emerged in response to police violence and systemic racism against Black communities.

Campaigns: BLM activists organized protests, rallies, and social media campaigns to raise awareness of police brutality and advocate for racial justice.

Impact: The BLM movement has sparked national and global conversations about race, policing, and social inequality, leading to policy reforms, increased accountability for law enforcement, and a renewed commitment to addressing systemic racism.

3. #MeToo Movement

Overview

Context: The #MeToo movement originated as a campaign to raise awareness of sexual harassment and assault, particularly in the workplace.

Campaigns: Survivors and advocates shared their experiences of sexual misconduct using the hashtag #MeToo, leading to a wave of disclosures and public outrage.

Impact: The #MeToo movement has led to greater awareness of sexual harassment and assault, changes in corporate policies and workplace culture, and increased accountability for perpetrators in various industries.

4. Say Her Name

Overview

Context: The Say Her Name campaign was launched to raise awareness of police violence against Black women and girls, whose experiences are often overlooked in discussions of racial justice.

Campaigns: Activists organized rallies, social media campaigns, and artistic projects to honor and remember Black women and girls who have been killed by police.

Impact: Say Her Name has highlighted the intersection of race and gender in police violence, challenging stereotypes and amplifying the voices of Black women and girls in the fight for racial justice.

5. Standing Rock Protests

Overview

Context: The Standing Rock protests were a series of demonstrations against the construction of the Dakota Access Pipeline near the Standing Rock Indian Reservation.
Campaigns: Indigenous activists and allies organized encampments, legal challenges, and direct actions to protect land, water, and sacred sites from environmental destruction.
Impact: The Standing Rock protests galvanized support for Indigenous rights, environmental justice, and solidarity movements, drawing international attention to the impacts of fossil fuel infrastructure on Indigenous communities and the environment.
6. Anti-Apartheid Movement
Overview

Context: The anti-apartheid movement was a global campaign to end racial segregation and discrimination in South Africa.
Campaigns: Activists around the world organized boycotts, divestment campaigns, and protests to pressure the South African government to dismantle apartheid policies.
Impact: The anti-apartheid movement contributed to the release of Nelson Mandela, the end of apartheid, and the establishment of democratic governance in South Africa, demonstrating the power of international solidarity in the fight against racism and oppression.
Conclusion
These case studies illustrate the power of racial justice campaigns to challenge systemic racism, amplify marginalized voices, and mobilize communities for social change. By learning from the successes and strategies of past and ongoing movements, we can continue to build momentum towards a more just, equitable, and inclusive society for all. This chapter emphasizes the importance of collective action, solidarity, and sustained advocacy in the pursuit of racial justice and human rights.

Chapter 12: Immigration and Border Issues: Historical Trends in Immigration Policies

Introduction
Immigration and border issues have long been contentious topics, shaped by historical trends, political ideologies, and socio-economic factors. This chapter explores the evolution of immigration policies over time, tracing key developments and their impact on immigrant communities and border regions.

Early Immigration Policies
*1. Colonial Era

During the colonial era, immigration to North America was largely unregulated, with European settlers arriving in search of land, religious freedom, and economic opportunity. Indigenous peoples were displaced and marginalized as European colonization expanded, leading to centuries of conflict, dispossession, and forced assimilation.
**2. Chinese Exclusion Act

In the late 19th century, the United States enacted the Chinese Exclusion Act, which barred Chinese laborers from immigrating to the country.
The law reflected anti-Chinese sentiment and fears of economic competition, leading to decades of discrimination and exclusionary policies targeting Chinese immigrants.
Immigration Reform and National Origins Quotas
*1. Immigration Act of 1924

The Immigration Act of 1924 established national origins quotas that restricted immigration from certain countries, particularly those in Southern and Eastern Europe, Asia, and Africa.
The law favored immigrants from Northern and Western Europe, reflecting nativist attitudes and racial hierarchies prevalent at the time.
**2. Bracero Program

During World War II, the United States implemented the Bracero Program, which allowed temporary guest workers from Mexico to fill labor shortages in agriculture and other industries.
The program exposed migrant workers to exploitation and abuse, while also contributing to the growth of Mexican immigrant communities in the United States.
Civil Rights Era and Immigration Reform
*1. Immigration and Nationality Act of 1965

The Immigration and Nationality Act of 1965 abolished the national origins quotas system and established a new immigration policy based on family reunification and skilled labor.
The law led to a surge in immigration from Latin America, Asia, and other regions, diversifying the immigrant population and reshaping American demographics.
**2. Refugee Resettlement

In the aftermath of World War II and subsequent conflicts, the United States implemented refugee resettlement programs to provide protection and assistance to displaced persons.
Refugees from Vietnam, Cambodia, Laos, and other countries found refuge in the United States, contributing to the growth of refugee communities and enriching American society.
Contemporary Immigration Policies
*1. Immigration Reform and Control Act of 1986

The Immigration Reform and Control Act of 1986 granted amnesty to undocumented immigrants who had been living in the United States since before 1982 and imposed sanctions on employers who hired unauthorized workers.

The law failed to address root causes of undocumented immigration and contributed to the growth of unauthorized migration in subsequent decades.

**2. Deferred Action for Childhood Arrivals (DACA)

In 2012, the Obama administration implemented DACA, which provided temporary relief from deportation and work authorization to undocumented immigrants who were brought to the United States as children.

DACA recipients, known as Dreamers, have become vocal advocates for immigration reform and pathways to citizenship for undocumented immigrants.

Conclusion

The history of immigration policies reflects a complex interplay of economic interests, political ideologies, and social attitudes towards immigrants and border communities. By understanding historical trends and policy legacies, we can better appreciate the challenges and opportunities facing immigrant communities today and work towards more humane, equitable, and inclusive immigration policies in the future. This chapter underscores the importance of addressing systemic injustices and upholding the rights and dignity of all individuals, regardless of their immigration status or background.

Chapter 13: Current Refugee Crises and Humanitarian Responses: Analysis of Border Control Policies

Introduction
The world is facing unprecedented refugee crises, driven by conflicts, persecution, and environmental disasters. This chapter examines the current refugee crises and humanitarian responses, while analyzing the border control policies that shape the experiences of refugees and migrants seeking safety and protection.

Current Refugee Crises
*1. Syrian Refugee Crisis

The ongoing conflict in Syria has resulted in one of the largest refugee crises of the 21st century, with millions of Syrians fleeing violence, persecution, and displacement.
Syrian refugees have sought refuge in neighboring countries, Europe, and beyond, facing significant challenges and barriers to protection and resettlement.
**2. Rohingya Refugee Crisis

The persecution of Rohingya Muslims in Myanmar has forced hundreds of thousands of Rohingya to flee to neighboring Bangladesh and other countries in Southeast Asia.
Rohingya refugees have faced dire conditions in overcrowded refugee camps, with limited access to basic necessities and protection from violence and exploitation.

Humanitarian Responses
*1. International Aid and Assistance

Humanitarian organizations, governments, and NGOs have
mobilized to provide emergency aid, shelter, healthcare, and
support services to refugees and displaced populations.
Efforts to address the root causes of displacement, promote
peacebuilding, and facilitate durable solutions are also
underway.
**2. Resettlement and Integration

Resettlement programs offer refugees the opportunity to
rebuild their lives in third countries, providing pathways to
citizenship, education, employment, and social integration.
Community-based initiatives and grassroots efforts support
refugee integration and foster solidarity and empathy among
host communities.
Analysis of Border Control Policies
*1. Securitization and Militarization

Border control policies in many countries have become
increasingly securitized and militarized, prioritizing national
security and deterrence over humanitarian protection.
Measures such as border walls, detention centers, and
heightened surveillance have restricted access to asylum and
subjected refugees and migrants to violence, exploitation, and
human rights abuses.
**2. Refugee Protection and Legal Pathways

Effective border control policies should prioritize refugee
protection, uphold international law, and ensure access to
asylum procedures for those fleeing persecution and violence.
Legal pathways for migration, such as resettlement programs,
family reunification, and humanitarian visas, provide
alternatives to irregular migration and dangerous journeys.
Challenges and Opportunities

*1. Global Solidarity

Addressing refugee crises requires collective action, global solidarity, and burden-sharing among countries, regions, and international organizations.
Cooperation on refugee protection, resettlement, and integration can enhance humanitarian responses and promote more equitable solutions to displacement.
**2. Human Rights and Dignity

Upholding human rights and dignity should be central to border control policies and practices, ensuring that refugees and migrants are treated with respect, compassion, and fairness.
Advocacy efforts, legal advocacy, and public awareness campaigns can hold governments accountable for their obligations to protect the rights of refugees and uphold humanitarian principles.
Conclusion
The current refugee crises present complex challenges and moral imperatives for the international community. By addressing the root causes of displacement, providing humanitarian assistance, and adopting more humane and rights-based border control policies, we can work towards a more just, compassionate, and inclusive world for refugees and migrants. This chapter emphasizes the importance of solidarity, empathy, and collective action in responding to refugee crises and upholding the rights and dignity of all people, regardless of their nationality or immigration status.

Chapter 14: Case Studies: Stories from the Frontlines

Introduction
Behind every statistic, policy, and headline are real people with unique experiences and struggles. This chapter shares compelling stories from the frontlines of immigration, refugee crises, and border control, highlighting the human impact of these complex issues.

1. Ahmed's Journey: Escaping War in Syria
Ahmed, a young Syrian refugee, fled his war-torn homeland with his family in search of safety and stability. Their journey was fraught with peril, as they navigated dangerous routes, faced exploitation by smugglers, and endured hardship along the way. Despite the challenges, Ahmed's resilience and determination to build a better future for his family inspire hope amid adversity.

2. Maria's Dream: Seeking Asylum in the United States
Maria, a transgender woman from Honduras, fled persecution and violence in her home country due to her gender identity. Seeking asylum in the United States, Maria embarked on a harrowing journey filled with uncertainty and fear. Along the way, she encountered obstacles, discrimination, and violence, yet remained steadfast in her pursuit of safety and acceptance.

3. Jamal's Struggle: Surviving the Rohingya Genocide

Jamal, a Rohingya refugee, narrowly escaped a brutal crackdown in Myanmar that targeted his community for ethnic cleansing. Forced to flee his village with nothing but the clothes on his back, Jamal embarked on a perilous journey to Bangladesh in search of refuge. Despite the trauma and loss he endured, Jamal remains determined to rebuild his life and seek justice for his people.

4. Ana's Resilience: Navigating the Central American Migrant Caravan

Ana, a single mother from El Salvador, joined a migrant caravan bound for the United States in search of safety and opportunity for her children. Along the journey, Ana faced numerous challenges, including violence, exploitation, and separation from her loved ones. Despite the risks, Ana's courage and resilience sustain her as she continues her quest for a better life.

5. Mustafa's Hope: Rebuilding in a Refugee Camp

Mustafa, a Syrian refugee, found himself living in a crowded refugee camp in Jordan after fleeing the violence in his homeland. Despite the harsh conditions and limited resources, Mustafa refused to lose hope. Through education, community support, and his own resilience, Mustafa began to rebuild his life and pursue his dreams of a brighter future.

Conclusion

These stories offer a glimpse into the lived experiences of individuals and families who have been directly impacted by immigration, refugee crises, and border control policies. By sharing their stories, we honor their courage, resilience, and humanity, while also recognizing the urgent need for compassionate and effective responses to the challenges they face. This chapter underscores the importance of empathy, solidarity, and advocacy in advancing justice and dignity for all people, regardless of their background or circumstances.

Chapter 15: Political Polarization: Causes of Political Division in Modern Societies

Introduction
Political polarization has become a defining feature of modern societies, leading to deep divisions and heightened tensions among individuals and communities. This chapter explores the complex causes of political polarization, examining the societal, cultural, and structural factors that contribute to the widening ideological gap.

1. Media Fragmentation and Echo Chambers
*1. Partisan Media Outlets

The rise of partisan media outlets and social media platforms has contributed to the fragmentation of information and the creation of ideological echo chambers.
Individuals are increasingly exposed to content that reinforces their existing beliefs and biases, leading to a lack of exposure to diverse perspectives and alternative viewpoints.
**2. Filter Bubbles and Algorithmic Bias

Algorithmic algorithms used by social media platforms and search engines prioritize content based on user preferences, leading to the creation of filter bubbles that reinforce ideological divides.

Individuals are less likely to encounter opposing viewpoints or challenging information, further entrenching their ideological positions and exacerbating polarization.

2. Identity Politics and Group Affiliation

*1. Social Identity Theory

Social identity theory posits that individuals derive their sense of self-worth and belonging from membership in social groups, such as political parties, religious affiliations, or cultural identities.

Group identities can become politicized and polarized, leading to ingroup favoritism, outgroup hostility, and the demonization of political opponents.

**2. Polarization by Proxy

Political elites and media figures often exploit identity-based grievances and cultural anxieties to mobilize support and galvanize political movements.

Issues such as immigration, race, religion, and national identity are frequently weaponized for political gain, further dividing society along ideological lines.

3. Economic Inequality and Discontent

*1. Widening Wealth Gap

Economic inequality and stagnating wages have fueled public discontent and resentment towards political and economic elites.

Perceptions of unfairness and injustice in the distribution of wealth and opportunity can drive populist movements and anti-establishment sentiment.

**2. Cultural Backlash

Economic anxieties and cultural insecurities are often intertwined, leading to a sense of cultural backlash against globalization, multiculturalism, and social change.
Populist leaders and nationalist movements exploit these anxieties to mobilize support and scapegoat marginalized groups, further polarizing society along cultural and ideological lines.
4. Political Gerrymandering and Electoral Systems
*1. Partisan Gerrymandering

Political gerrymandering, the practice of redrawing electoral districts to favor one political party over another, has distorted representation and entrenched incumbents.
Gerrymandered districts often produce hyperpartisan politicians who cater to the ideological extremes of their base, exacerbating political polarization.
**2. Polarized Electoral Systems

Electoral systems that incentivize winner-takes-all outcomes, such as first-past-the-post voting, can exacerbate political polarization by marginalizing third parties and reinforcing a two-party duopoly.
Polarized electoral systems can lead to zero-sum politics, where compromise and cooperation are viewed as signs of weakness rather than essential components of democratic governance.
Conclusion
Political polarization is a multifaceted phenomenon driven by a combination of societal, cultural, and structural factors. By understanding the root causes of polarization, we can begin to address the underlying dynamics and work towards fostering greater empathy, understanding, and cooperation across ideological divides. This chapter underscores the importance of promoting civic engagement, media literacy, and inclusive political discourse in mitigating the harmful effects of polarization and strengthening democratic institutions.

Chapter 16: Impact of Polarization on Governance and Society: Strategies for Bridging the Divide

Introduction
The growing polarization of political discourse has profound implications for governance, social cohesion, and democratic norms. This chapter examines the impact of polarization on governance and society, while exploring strategies for overcoming ideological divides and fostering greater unity and cooperation.

1. Erosion of Trust in Institutions
*1. Decline in Political Trust

Political polarization has eroded public trust in government institutions, political leaders, and democratic processes. Skepticism towards mainstream media, scientific expertise, and the rule of law has further undermined confidence in the foundations of democratic governance.
**2. Polarized Governance

Political gridlock and partisan polarization have hampered legislative effectiveness and hindered policymaking on critical issues.

Divided government and hyperpartisanship have led to legislative stalemates, government shutdowns, and a lack of consensus on pressing challenges such as healthcare, immigration, and climate change.

2. Social Fragmentation and Identity Politics

*1. Social Fragmentation

Political polarization has contributed to social fragmentation and the erosion of social cohesion, as individuals increasingly self-segregate into like-minded communities.

Social media algorithms and echo chambers exacerbate divisions, leading to echo chambers and ideological bubbles that reinforce partisan identities and isolate individuals from diverse perspectives.

**2. Identity-Based Politics

Identity politics, fueled by polarization, has intensified group conflicts and heightened tensions along racial, ethnic, religious, and cultural lines.

Identity-based grievances are often exploited by political elites to mobilize support and galvanize political movements, further polarizing society and undermining efforts to bridge ideological divides.

3. Strategies for Bridging the Divide

*1. Promoting Civil Discourse and Dialogue

Encouraging respectful and constructive dialogue across ideological divides can help foster understanding, empathy, and cooperation.

Platforms for civic engagement, community forums, and intergroup dialogue initiatives provide opportunities for meaningful engagement and bridge-building.

**2. Fostering Media Literacy

Promoting media literacy and critical thinking skills can empower individuals to navigate information ecosystems, discern fact from fiction, and resist manipulation by partisan narratives.

Educational initiatives and media literacy campaigns can equip citizens with the tools to critically evaluate news sources, challenge misinformation, and engage in informed civic discourse.

**3. Building Coalitions and Compromise

Building coalitions across ideological lines and finding common ground on shared values and priorities can facilitate bipartisan cooperation and consensus-building.

Emphasizing pragmatism and compromise over ideological purity can help break through gridlock and advance practical solutions to pressing challenges.

**4. Investing in Civic Education and Participation

Investing in civic education programs and initiatives can cultivate informed and engaged citizens who are equipped to participate meaningfully in democratic processes.

Empowering marginalized communities, promoting voter registration and turnout, and expanding access to political participation can help ensure that diverse voices are represented in governance.

Conclusion

Political polarization poses significant challenges to governance, social cohesion, and democratic legitimacy. However, by adopting strategies for bridging the ideological divide, fostering constructive dialogue, and promoting civic engagement, societies can mitigate the harmful effects of polarization and build a more resilient and inclusive democracy. This chapter underscores the importance of collective action, empathy, and cooperation in addressing the root causes of polarization and advancing the common good.

Chapter 17: Case Studies: Efforts to Reduce Polarization

Introduction
In the face of growing political polarization, individuals and organizations around the world are undertaking innovative initiatives to promote dialogue, understanding, and cooperation across ideological divides. This chapter highlights case studies of efforts to reduce polarization, offering insights into effective strategies and promising approaches.

1. The Better Angels Movement
*1. Mission and Approach

The Better Angels Movement seeks to depolarize America by bringing together individuals from across the political spectrum for structured dialogues and workshops. Through facilitated discussions and empathy-building exercises, participants learn to listen to opposing viewpoints with respect and understanding, fostering mutual appreciation and constructive engagement.
**2. Impact and Outcomes

The Better Angels Movement has successfully facilitated hundreds of workshops and dialogues across the United States, reaching thousands of participants from diverse backgrounds.

Participants report increased empathy, reduced animosity towards political opponents, and a greater sense of common humanity, paving the way for bridging ideological divides and building trust across communities.

2. BridgeUSA: Bridging the Partisan Divide on College Campuses

*1. Student-Led Initiative

BridgeUSA is a student-led organization that promotes civil discourse and political diversity on college campuses. Through events, debates, and dialogue initiatives, BridgeUSA creates spaces for students with diverse political perspectives to engage in respectful and constructive discussions on contentious issues.

**2. Campus Chapters and Impact

BridgeUSA has established chapters at universities across the United States, fostering dialogue and engagement among students with differing political beliefs.

By providing platforms for open-minded inquiry and collaboration, BridgeUSA encourages students to transcend partisan divides and work towards common goals, both on campus and in society at large.

3. Essential Partners: Facilitating Difficult Conversations

*1. Dialogue Facilitation

Essential Partners (formerly Public Conversations Project) is a non-profit organization that specializes in facilitating constructive conversations on polarizing issues.

Trained facilitators work with diverse stakeholders to create safe spaces for dialogue, allowing participants to explore their differences, find common ground, and build relationships based on respect and understanding.
**2. Community Engagement and Conflict Resolution

Essential Partners has facilitated dialogues on a wide range of topics, including race, religion, politics, and identity, in communities across the United States and around the world. By fostering empathy, deep listening, and collaboration, Essential Partners helps communities navigate complex conflicts and find sustainable solutions that honor diverse perspectives and interests.
4. Living Room Conversations: Building Bridges One Conversation at a Time
*1. Structured Dialogue Framework

Living Room Conversations is a grassroots initiative that brings together individuals with differing political viewpoints for small-group discussions in private homes and community spaces.
Using a structured dialogue framework, participants explore predetermined topics, share personal experiences and perspectives, and seek common ground on issues of mutual concern.
**2. Community Building and Empowerment

Living Room Conversations has facilitated thousands of conversations across the United States, fostering connections and relationships among individuals with diverse backgrounds and beliefs.
By emphasizing listening, curiosity, and respect, Living Room Conversations empowers participants to transcend ideological divides and build bridges of understanding and cooperation within their communities.
Conclusion

These case studies demonstrate the power of dialogue, empathy, and collaboration in reducing political polarization and building bridges across divides. By creating opportunities for respectful engagement, fostering understanding, and nurturing common ground, these initiatives offer hope for a more united and inclusive society. This chapter underscores the importance of grassroots efforts, community engagement, and collective action in addressing the root causes of polarization and strengthening democratic values.

Chapter 18: Globalization: Impacts and Challenges

Introduction
Globalization, the interconnectedness of economies, cultures, and societies across borders, has transformed the world in profound ways. This chapter explores the impacts and challenges of globalization, examining its effects on economies, cultures, and the environment, as well as the opportunities and risks it presents for individuals and communities worldwide.

1. Economic Globalization
*1. Trade and Investment

Economic globalization has facilitated the expansion of trade and investment flows, leading to increased economic interdependence among nations.

Global supply chains and international trade agreements have driven economic growth, innovation, and prosperity, while also exposing economies to risks and vulnerabilities.
**2. Income Inequality

While globalization has contributed to overall economic growth, it has also exacerbated income inequality within and between countries.
Unequal distribution of wealth and opportunities has fueled social tensions and political polarization, undermining social cohesion and stability.
2. Cultural Globalization
*1. Cultural Exchange and Diversity

Cultural globalization has led to the exchange of ideas, values, and cultural practices across borders, enriching societies with diverse perspectives and experiences.
The spread of digital technology and social media has democratized access to information and facilitated cross-cultural dialogue and collaboration.
**2. Cultural Homogenization

Despite the diversity of cultural expressions, globalization has also led to concerns about cultural homogenization and the erosion of local traditions and identities.
Western cultural dominance, fueled by media conglomerates and global brands, has raised questions about cultural imperialism and the preservation of cultural heritage.
3. Environmental Globalization
*1. Resource Extraction and Pollution

Globalization has intensified resource extraction and production processes, leading to environmental degradation and pollution.

Industrialization, deforestation, and urbanization have contributed to climate change, biodiversity loss, and ecosystem destruction, posing existential threats to the planet.
**2. Global Cooperation on Environmental Issues

Despite the challenges posed by globalization, it has also fostered global cooperation on environmental issues through international agreements and initiatives.
Efforts to address climate change, protect endangered species, and promote sustainable development require collective action and cooperation among nations.
4. Social Globalization
*1. Migration and Diaspora Communities

Social globalization has facilitated human mobility, migration, and the formation of diaspora communities around the world. Migrants contribute to cultural diversity, economic development, and social innovation in their host countries, while also facing challenges related to integration and social cohesion.
**2. Global Challenges and Solidarity

Globalization has interconnected societies in unprecedented ways, highlighting the need for solidarity and cooperation in addressing global challenges such as pandemics, poverty, and human rights violations.
Efforts to promote social justice, human dignity, and equitable development require cross-border collaboration and shared responsibility.
Conclusion

Globalization has reshaped the world in complex and interconnected ways, bringing both opportunities and challenges for individuals, communities, and nations. By understanding the multifaceted impacts of globalization and addressing its associated risks, societies can harness its potential to promote sustainable development, foster cultural exchange, and build a more equitable and inclusive world. This chapter underscores the importance of collective action, global cooperation, and ethical governance in navigating the complexities of globalization and shaping a future that benefits all humanity.

Chapter 19: Definition and History of Globalization: Economic, Political, and Cultural Impacts

Introduction

Globalization, the process of increasing interconnectedness and interdependence among countries and regions, has profoundly shaped the modern world. This chapter provides an overview of the definition and history of globalization, examining its economic, political, and cultural impacts on societies around the globe.

1. Definition of Globalization
*1. Interconnectedness and Interdependence

Globalization refers to the intensification of economic, political, cultural, and social interactions across borders, facilitated by advances in technology, communication, and transportation.
It involves the flow of goods, services, capital, information, ideas, and people across national boundaries, blurring distinctions between local and global phenomena.
**2. Dimensions of Globalization

Economic globalization encompasses the integration of markets, production processes, and financial systems on a global scale.
Political globalization involves the expansion of international institutions, governance structures, and diplomatic relations to address global challenges and opportunities.
Cultural globalization refers to the exchange of ideas, values, beliefs, and cultural practices across diverse societies, leading to the emergence of global cultural flows and hybrid identities.
2. Historical Origins of Globalization
*1. Trade and Exchange Networks

Globalization has deep historical roots, dating back to ancient trade routes such as the Silk Road, which facilitated the exchange of goods, ideas, and cultures between Europe, Asia, and Africa.

The Age of Exploration and European colonization expanded global trade networks, leading to the exchange of commodities, technology, and knowledge between continents.
**2. Industrial Revolution

The Industrial Revolution in the 18th and 19th centuries transformed global economies and societies, fueling technological innovations, urbanization, and mass production. The rise of industrial capitalism and colonial empires laid the groundwork for modern globalization, as goods, capital, and labor flowed between continents in unprecedented volumes.
3. Economic Impacts of Globalization
*1. Trade and Investment

Economic globalization has led to the expansion of international trade and investment flows, driving economic growth, innovation, and specialization.
Global supply chains and outsourcing have reshaped global production networks, leading to the relocation of manufacturing and service industries to low-cost labor markets.
**2. Income Inequality and Labor Market Changes

While globalization has generated overall economic gains, it has also contributed to income inequality within and between countries.
The outsourcing of jobs, technological automation, and wage stagnation have disproportionately affected low-skilled workers and marginalized communities, exacerbating social disparities.
4. Political Impacts of Globalization
*1. Global Governance and Institutions

Political globalization has led to the emergence of international institutions, multilateral agreements, and diplomatic frameworks to address global challenges such as climate change, pandemics, and security threats.
Organizations such as the United Nations, World Bank, International Monetary Fund, and World Trade Organization play key roles in shaping global governance and cooperation.
**2. National Sovereignty and Transnationalism

Globalization has challenged traditional notions of national sovereignty and territorial borders, as governments grapple with transnational issues such as migration, terrorism, and cybercrime.
The rise of supranational entities and regional blocs, such as the European Union, reflects efforts to navigate the complexities of global interdependence while preserving national autonomy.
5. Cultural Impacts of Globalization
*1. Cultural Exchange and Hybridization

Cultural globalization has led to the exchange of ideas, values, and cultural practices across diverse societies, fostering cultural hybridization and the emergence of global cultural flows.
The spread of digital technology, social media, and mass media has facilitated cross-cultural communication and interaction, shaping shared norms, tastes, and identities.
**2. Cultural Imperialism and Resistance

Despite the diversity of cultural expressions, globalization has also led to concerns about cultural imperialism and the homogenization of local cultures.
Western cultural dominance, facilitated by media conglomerates and global brands, has prompted backlash and resistance from communities seeking to preserve their cultural heritage and identities.

Conclusion
Globalization is a multifaceted phenomenon that has reshaped economies, politics, and cultures on a global scale. By examining its historical origins and multifaceted impacts, we gain insights into the opportunities and challenges it presents for societies around the world. This chapter underscores the importance of understanding globalization as a complex and dynamic process, shaped by diverse forces and actors, and highlights the need for informed dialogue and cooperation to navigate its complexities and harness its potential for the benefit of all humanity.

Chapter 20: Benefits and Challenges of Globalization

Introduction

Globalization has transformed the world in profound ways, bringing both opportunities and challenges for individuals, communities, and nations. This chapter examines the benefits and challenges of globalization, exploring its impact on economies, societies, and the environment, as well as the implications for human well-being and development.

1. Economic Benefits
*1. Increased Trade and Investment

Globalization has expanded international trade and investment flows, opening up new markets, promoting economic growth, and creating opportunities for businesses to thrive in a global marketplace.
Access to foreign markets and resources has facilitated specialization, innovation, and efficiency gains, leading to higher productivity and living standards.
**2. Technological Innovation

Advances in technology and communication have accelerated the pace of globalization, enabling instant connectivity, information sharing, and collaboration across borders.
Digital technologies, automation, and artificial intelligence have revolutionized industries, driving productivity gains, cost efficiencies, and new business models.
2. Social and Cultural Benefits
*1. Cultural Exchange and Diversity

Globalization has facilitated the exchange of ideas, values, and cultural practices across diverse societies, enriching global cultural diversity and fostering cross-cultural understanding.
Cultural globalization has led to the emergence of hybrid identities, cultural fusion, and global cultural movements that transcend national borders and promote inclusivity and diversity.
**2. Humanitarian Aid and Global Solidarity

Globalization has facilitated international cooperation and solidarity in addressing humanitarian crises, natural disasters, and public health emergencies.
Humanitarian organizations, governments, and civil society actors collaborate to provide humanitarian aid, disaster relief, and development assistance to vulnerable populations around the world.
3. Environmental Benefits
*1. Global Environmental Cooperation

Globalization has fostered cooperation among nations in addressing environmental challenges such as climate change, biodiversity loss, and pollution.
International agreements and initiatives promote sustainable development, environmental conservation, and the transition to clean energy, transcending national boundaries and fostering global environmental stewardship.
**2. Technological Solutions

Technological innovations and scientific advancements offer solutions to environmental problems, such as renewable energy technologies, sustainable agriculture practices, and eco-friendly manufacturing processes.
Global collaboration on research and development accelerates the deployment of green technologies and promotes sustainable resource management practices.
4. Economic, Social, and Environmental Challenges
*1. Income Inequality and Economic Disparities

Despite the overall economic gains from globalization, it has also contributed to widening income inequality within and between countries.
Economic disparities, job displacement, and social exclusion exacerbate social tensions and undermine inclusive development, particularly in marginalized communities.

**2. Cultural Homogenization and Identity Loss

Globalization has led to concerns about cultural homogenization and the erosion of local traditions, languages, and identities.
Western cultural dominance, fueled by media globalization and consumerism, marginalizes indigenous cultures and threatens cultural diversity and heritage.
*3. Environmental Degradation and Resource Depletion

Globalization has intensified resource extraction, industrial pollution, and habitat destruction, leading to environmental degradation and ecosystem collapse.
Unsustainable consumption patterns, deforestation, and overexploitation of natural resources exacerbate climate change, biodiversity loss, and environmental crises.
Conclusion
Globalization presents a complex array of benefits and challenges for individuals, societies, and the planet. By harnessing its potential for economic development, cultural exchange, and environmental sustainability, societies can strive towards a more equitable, inclusive, and resilient global community. This chapter underscores the importance of addressing the challenges of globalization, mitigating its negative impacts, and maximizing its benefits for the well-being of present and future generations.

Chapter 21: Case Studies: Globalization's Effects on Local Communities

Introduction
Globalization has profound effects on local communities around the world, shaping economies, cultures, and social dynamics in diverse ways. This chapter presents case studies that illustrate the impacts of globalization on local communities, highlighting both the opportunities and challenges they face in a rapidly changing globalized world.

1. Impact of Globalization on Local Economies: Rust Belt Communities in the United States
*1. Case Study: Rust Belt Cities

Rust Belt cities in the United States, once thriving industrial centers, have experienced economic decline and job loss due to globalization and deindustrialization.
The outsourcing of manufacturing jobs to low-cost labor markets overseas, coupled with technological automation, has led to factory closures, unemployment, and urban blight in communities such as Detroit, Cleveland, and Pittsburgh.
**2. Community Responses

Rust Belt communities have responded to economic challenges by diversifying their economies, investing in education and workforce development, and fostering entrepreneurship and innovation.

Revitalization efforts, such as adaptive reuse of industrial sites, downtown redevelopment, and investment in arts and culture, aim to revitalize local economies and create new opportunities for growth and resilience.

2. Cultural Impacts of Globalization: Indigenous Communities in the Amazon Rainforest

*1. Case Study: Indigenous Tribes in the Amazon

Indigenous communities in the Amazon rainforest face cultural, social, and environmental threats from globalization, including deforestation, land grabbing, and encroachment by extractive industries.

Global demand for commodities such as timber, minerals, and agricultural products drives environmental degradation and threatens the traditional livelihoods and cultural heritage of indigenous peoples.

**2. Community Resistance and Resilience

Indigenous communities in the Amazon have organized grassroots movements, protests, and legal battles to defend their land rights, protect their territories, and preserve their cultural identity and way of life.

Community-led initiatives, such as ecotourism, sustainable forestry, and artisanal crafts, offer alternative economic opportunities that support cultural preservation and environmental conservation.

3. Social Impacts of Globalization: Urban Gentrification in Global Cities

*1. Case Study: Gentrification in Global Cities

Gentrification, driven by globalization and urbanization, has transformed neighborhoods in global cities such as London, New York, and Tokyo, leading to displacement, social inequality, and cultural displacement.

Rising property values, luxury development projects, and influx of affluent residents push out long-time residents, small businesses, and cultural institutions, exacerbating social divisions and eroding community cohesion.

**2. Community Resistance and Advocacy

Local residents, activists, and community organizations have mobilized to resist gentrification and advocate for affordable housing, tenant rights, and equitable development policies. Grassroots movements, community land trusts, and participatory planning initiatives seek to empower residents, preserve neighborhood character, and promote inclusive urban development that benefits all members of the community.

Conclusion

These case studies highlight the diverse ways in which globalization impacts local communities, shaping their economies, cultures, and social dynamics. By understanding the specific challenges and opportunities faced by local communities in a globalized world, policymakers, practitioners, and stakeholders can develop more informed and context-specific strategies to promote sustainable development, social justice, and community resilience. This chapter underscores the importance of community engagement, local empowerment, and cross-sector collaboration in addressing the impacts of globalization and building more inclusive and resilient communities for the future.

Chapter 22: Economic Inequality: Causes, Consequences, and Solutions

Introduction
Economic inequality, the unequal distribution of wealth and income within and between societies, is a pressing global challenge with far-reaching implications for social cohesion, economic stability, and human development. This chapter examines the causes, consequences, and potential solutions to economic inequality, offering insights into strategies for promoting greater equity and opportunity for all.

1. Causes of Economic Inequality
*1. Structural Factors

Structural factors such as globalization, technological change, and economic policies contribute to the concentration of wealth and power in the hands of a few.
Globalization leads to outsourcing of jobs, while technological advances automate tasks, displacing workers and widening the gap between skilled and unskilled labor.
**2. Policy Choices

Policy choices, such as tax policies, deregulation, and austerity measures, can exacerbate economic inequality by favoring the wealthy and reducing social safety nets for the poor.
Tax cuts for the rich, corporate subsidies, and regressive taxation schemes widen the wealth gap and undermine public services that benefit the most vulnerable.
2. Consequences of Economic Inequality
*1. Social Cohesion and Stability

Economic inequality undermines social cohesion and stability by creating resentment, alienation, and mistrust between different socioeconomic groups.
Rising inequality can lead to social unrest, political polarization, and erosion of democratic institutions, threatening social peace and economic progress.
**2. Health and Well-being

Economic inequality has detrimental effects on health outcomes, life expectancy, and overall well-being, particularly for low-income individuals and marginalized communities.
Health disparities, lack of access to healthcare, and stress-related illnesses are more prevalent in societies with high levels of economic inequality.
3. Solutions to Economic Inequality
*1. Progressive Taxation and Redistribution

Progressive taxation, where the wealthy pay a higher proportion of their income in taxes, can help reduce economic inequality and fund social programs that benefit the poor.
Policies such as universal basic income, wealth taxes, and inheritance taxes can redistribute wealth and promote greater economic fairness.
**2. Investment in Education and Skills Development

Investment in education and skills development is crucial for reducing economic inequality by providing individuals with opportunities to improve their earning potential and social mobility.

Access to quality education, vocational training, and lifelong learning programs can empower individuals to compete in the global economy and secure higher-paying jobs.

**3. Labor Market Reforms and Worker Protections

Labor market reforms, such as minimum wage laws, collective bargaining rights, and worker protections, can help address wage stagnation and precarious employment.

Policies that promote fair wages, job security, and decent working conditions empower workers and reduce economic disparities between labor and capital.

Conclusion

Economic inequality is a complex and multifaceted issue that requires comprehensive and coordinated responses at the global, national, and local levels. By addressing the root causes of inequality, promoting equitable policies, and investing in human capital and social protection, societies can create more inclusive and sustainable economies that benefit everyone. This chapter underscores the importance of political will, social solidarity, and collective action in tackling economic inequality and building a more just and prosperous world for future generations.

Chapter 23: Examination of Wealth Disparity and its Roots: Impact of Economic Policies on Poverty

Introduction
Wealth disparity, the unequal distribution of assets and resources within a society, is a pervasive issue with deep-rooted causes and far-reaching consequences. This chapter delves into the examination of wealth disparity and its underlying roots, focusing on the impact of economic policies on poverty levels. By understanding the complexities of wealth inequality and the role of policy interventions, we can explore avenues for promoting greater equity and social justice.

1. Understanding Wealth Disparity
*1. Structural Inequities

Wealth disparity arises from structural inequities in access to resources, opportunities, and power within society.

Historical legacies of colonialism, slavery, and discriminatory policies have perpetuated intergenerational wealth gaps and systemic barriers to economic mobility.
**2. Economic Systems

Economic systems, such as capitalism and neoliberalism, can exacerbate wealth disparity by prioritizing profit maximization and wealth accumulation for the few over equitable distribution of resources for all.
Market deregulation, privatization, and austerity measures often disproportionately benefit the wealthy while leaving the poor and marginalized behind.
2. Impact of Economic Policies on Poverty
*1. Income Redistribution

Economic policies play a significant role in shaping wealth distribution and poverty levels within society.
Progressive taxation, social welfare programs, and targeted poverty alleviation measures can help redistribute income and wealth to reduce poverty and inequality.
**2. Labor Market Regulations

Labor market policies, such as minimum wage laws, employment protections, and collective bargaining rights, influence income levels and working conditions for low-wage workers.
Fair labor standards and social protections can help lift workers out of poverty and ensure dignified livelihoods for all.
**3. Social Safety Nets

Social safety nets, including unemployment benefits, healthcare coverage, and housing assistance, serve as critical buffers against poverty and economic insecurity.

Strong social safety nets provide essential support for vulnerable populations, helping to prevent individuals and families from falling into poverty during times of crisis.
3. Addressing the Roots of Wealth Disparity
*1. Investment in Education and Skills Development

Education is a key determinant of economic opportunity and social mobility, yet access to quality education remains unequal across socioeconomic lines.
Investing in universal education, vocational training, and lifelong learning opportunities can empower individuals to escape the cycle of poverty and contribute to economic growth.
**2. Promoting Financial Inclusion

Financial inclusion initiatives, such as access to affordable credit, savings accounts, and microfinance services, can help marginalized communities build assets and escape poverty traps.
By promoting financial literacy and expanding access to banking services, governments can empower individuals to participate more fully in the formal economy and access economic opportunities.
**3. Supporting Sustainable Development

Policies that promote sustainable development, environmental conservation, and equitable resource management are essential for addressing the root causes of poverty and wealth disparity.
Investing in green technologies, renewable energy, and climate-resilient infrastructure can create new job opportunities, reduce economic vulnerability, and promote inclusive growth.
Conclusion

Wealth disparity is a complex and multifaceted issue that requires comprehensive and targeted policy responses to address its underlying roots and consequences. By examining the impact of economic policies on poverty levels and promoting inclusive and sustainable development strategies, societies can work towards building a more equitable and prosperous future for all. This chapter underscores the importance of political will, social solidarity, and collective action in tackling wealth disparity and advancing social justice and human dignity.

Chapter 24: Proposals for Economic Reforms: Towards a More Just and Inclusive Economy

Introduction
Economic reforms are essential for addressing the structural inequities and systemic injustices that perpetuate wealth disparity and hinder inclusive growth. This chapter presents a series of proposals for economic reforms aimed at creating a more just and inclusive economy. By implementing these reforms, societies can foster greater equity, opportunity, and prosperity for all citizens.

1. Progressive Taxation and Wealth Redistribution
*1. Introduction of Progressive Tax Rates

Implementing progressive tax rates that increase with income levels can ensure that the wealthiest individuals and corporations contribute a fair share of their earnings to support public goods and social programs.
This includes higher income tax rates for high-income earners, as well as wealth taxes on assets such as real estate, stocks, and inheritance.
**2. Closing Tax Loopholes and Offshore Tax Havens

Closing loopholes and cracking down on offshore tax havens can prevent tax evasion and ensure that corporations and high-net-worth individuals pay their fair share of taxes. Measures such as country-by-country reporting and automatic exchange of financial information can enhance transparency and accountability in the global financial system.
2. Strengthening Labor Protections and Social Safety Nets
*1. Raising Minimum Wage and Ensuring Living Wages

Raising the minimum wage to a level that ensures a living wage for all workers can help reduce poverty, increase consumer purchasing power, and stimulate economic growth. Indexing the minimum wage to inflation and productivity growth can ensure that wages keep pace with the cost of living and productivity gains over time.
**2. Expanding Access to Healthcare and Education

Guaranteeing universal access to quality healthcare and education is essential for promoting human capital development and social inclusion.
Implementing universal healthcare systems and tuition-free education policies can reduce disparities in access to essential services and empower individuals to reach their full potential.
3. Promoting Sustainable and Inclusive Growth
*1. Investing in Green Infrastructure and Clean Energy

Shifting towards a green economy by investing in renewable energy, sustainable transportation, and climate-resilient infrastructure can create millions of jobs while mitigating environmental risks.

Green investment strategies, such as carbon pricing and green bonds, can mobilize private capital towards sustainable development projects.

**2. Supporting Small and Medium-sized Enterprises (SMEs)

Providing targeted support for small and medium-sized enterprises (SMEs) can promote entrepreneurship, innovation, and inclusive economic growth.

Policies such as access to finance, technical assistance, and market support can help SMEs overcome barriers to growth and contribute to job creation and poverty reduction.

Conclusion

These proposals for economic reforms offer a roadmap for building a more just and inclusive economy that works for everyone. By implementing progressive taxation, strengthening labor protections, expanding social safety nets, and promoting sustainable and inclusive growth, societies can address the root causes of wealth disparity and advance towards a future of shared prosperity and opportunity. This chapter emphasizes the importance of political leadership, social dialogue, and collective action in driving meaningful economic reforms that benefit all members of society.

Chapter 25: Case Studies: Successful Initiatives to Reduce Inequality

Introduction
While wealth disparity and economic inequality pose significant challenges to societies worldwide, there are successful initiatives and strategies that have effectively reduced inequality and promoted greater equity and opportunity. This chapter examines case studies of such successful initiatives, highlighting lessons learned and best practices for addressing inequality.

1. Universal Basic Income: Finland's Experiment
*1. Case Study: Finland's Basic Income Experiment

Finland conducted a two-year basic income experiment from 2017 to 2019, providing 2,000 randomly selected unemployed citizens with a monthly basic income of 560 euros, regardless of employment status.
The experiment aimed to reduce poverty, bureaucracy, and unemployment traps, while promoting financial security and autonomy for participants.
**2. Outcomes and Lessons Learned

Preliminary findings suggested that basic income recipients experienced reduced stress, improved well-being, and increased trust in social institutions.
While the experiment did not significantly impact employment levels, it provided valuable insights into the potential of basic income as a tool for poverty alleviation and social protection.
2. Land Reform: South Korea's Saemaeul Undong Movement
*1. Case Study: Saemaeul Undong Movement

The Saemaeul Undong (New Village Movement) was a rural development initiative launched in South Korea in the 1970s to address poverty, inequality, and rural-urban disparities.
The movement focused on community-driven development, infrastructure improvement, agricultural modernization, and income generation projects in rural areas.
**2. Outcomes and Lessons Learned

The Saemaeul Undong significantly reduced rural poverty, increased agricultural productivity, and narrowed the gap between urban and rural incomes in South Korea.
Community participation, government support, and targeted investments in rural development were key factors contributing to the success of the movement.
3. Progressive Taxation and Wealth Redistribution: Nordic Model
*1. Case Study: Nordic Welfare States

Nordic countries such as Denmark, Sweden, Norway, and Finland have implemented progressive taxation systems, generous social welfare programs, and universal healthcare and education systems.

These policies aim to reduce inequality, promote social cohesion, and provide comprehensive social protection for all citizens.

**2. Outcomes and Lessons Learned

Nordic countries consistently rank among the lowest in terms of income inequality, poverty rates, and social disparities globally.

Progressive taxation, universal social benefits, and active labor market policies have contributed to high levels of social mobility, economic security, and quality of life in Nordic societies.

Conclusion

These case studies demonstrate that successful initiatives to reduce inequality are characterized by a combination of innovative policies, community participation, and political commitment. By learning from these examples and adopting evidence-based approaches, societies can effectively address the root causes of inequality and build more inclusive and resilient communities. This chapter underscores the importance of holistic and context-specific strategies for reducing inequality and promoting social justice and human dignity for all members of society.

Chapter 26: Gender Studies: Understanding Gender Equality and Equity

Introduction
Gender studies explore the social, cultural, and political dimensions of gender, examining the ways in which gender identity, roles, and norms shape individual experiences and societal structures. This chapter delves into the field of gender studies, highlighting key concepts, challenges, and strategies for achieving gender equality and equity.

1. Understanding Gender
*1. Gender as a Social Construct

Gender is a socially constructed concept that encompasses the roles, behaviors, expectations, and identities associated with being male, female, or non-binary.
Gender norms vary across cultures and historical contexts, influencing individual identities, relationships, and opportunities.
**2. Intersectionality and Gender Identity

Intersectionality examines how multiple social identities, such as race, class, sexuality, and disability, intersect and intersect with gender to shape experiences of privilege and oppression. Understanding intersectionality is essential for addressing the complex and intersecting forms of discrimination and marginalization faced by individuals with intersecting identities.
2. Gender Equality and Equity
*1. Gender Equality vs. Gender Equity

Gender equality refers to the equal rights, opportunities, and treatment of all genders, regardless of their biological sex or gender identity.
Gender equity goes beyond equality to address the systemic barriers and inequalities that prevent individuals from realizing their full potential and accessing resources and opportunities on equal terms.
**2. Challenges to Gender Equality

Persistent gender inequalities, such as wage gaps, gender-based violence, and limited political representation, continue to undermine gender equality efforts worldwide.
Patriarchal norms, stereotypes, and institutionalized discrimination perpetuate gender disparities and restrict women's and marginalized genders' access to rights and opportunities.
3. Strategies for Gender Empowerment

*1. Education and Awareness

Education and awareness-raising initiatives play a crucial role in challenging gender stereotypes, promoting gender equality, and empowering individuals to challenge discriminatory practices.
Comprehensive sexuality education, gender-sensitive curriculum, and media literacy programs can foster critical thinking and promote positive attitudes towards gender diversity.
**2. Policy Reforms and Legal Protections

Policy reforms and legal protections are essential for promoting gender equality and eliminating discrimination in all spheres of life.
Measures such as gender quotas, affirmative action policies, and anti-discrimination laws can help address structural barriers and promote representation and participation of women and marginalized genders in decision-making processes.
**3. Community Mobilization and Advocacy

Community mobilization and advocacy efforts are essential for raising awareness, building solidarity, and mobilizing collective action to advance gender equality.
Grassroots movements, women's rights organizations, and feminist activists play a critical role in challenging patriarchal norms, advocating for policy reforms, and holding governments and institutions accountable for gender equality commitments.
Conclusion

Gender studies offer valuable insights into the complex dynamics of gender inequality and the pathways to gender empowerment and social transformation. By promoting gender equality and equity, societies can create more inclusive, just, and sustainable futures for all individuals, regardless of their gender identity or expression. This chapter underscores the importance of intersectional approaches, policy reforms, and grassroots activism in advancing gender justice and human rights for all.

Chapter 27: History and Evolution of Feminism: Current Issues in Gender Identity and LGBTQ+ Rights

Introduction

The history and evolution of feminism trace the struggle for gender equality and the recognition of women's rights throughout the centuries. In tandem with feminism, the recognition and advocacy for LGBTQ+ rights have gained momentum, challenging societal norms and advocating for inclusivity. This chapter explores the rich history of feminism and the contemporary issues surrounding gender identity and LGBTQ+ rights.

1. History of Feminism
*1. First-wave Feminism

First-wave feminism emerged in the 19th and early 20th centuries, focusing on legal rights such as suffrage and property ownership for women.
Key figures such as Susan B. Anthony, Elizabeth Cady Stanton, and Emmeline Pankhurst led movements for women's rights and political representation.
**2. Second-wave Feminism

Second-wave feminism arose in the 1960s and 1970s, addressing systemic inequalities in areas such as education, employment, and reproductive rights.
Feminist activists like Betty Friedan, Gloria Steinem, and Audre Lorde advocated for gender equality and challenged traditional gender roles and stereotypes.
**3. Third-wave Feminism

Third-wave feminism emerged in the 1990s and focused on intersectionality, recognizing the diverse experiences of women based on race, class, sexuality, and other identities. Third-wave feminists emphasized inclusivity, LGBTQ+ rights, and the empowerment of marginalized voices within the feminist movement.
2. Current Issues in Gender Identity and LGBTQ+ Rights
*1. Gender Identity and Expression

Contemporary discussions on gender identity challenge binary notions of gender and recognize the fluidity and diversity of gender identities.
Movements such as transgender rights advocate for the recognition and protection of individuals' gender identity and expression.
**2. LGBTQ+ Rights

LGBTQ+ rights movements advocate for the rights and freedoms of lesbian, gay, bisexual, transgender, queer, and other marginalized identities.
Issues such as marriage equality, anti-discrimination protections, and healthcare access are central to LGBTQ+ advocacy efforts worldwide.
**3. Intersectionality and Inclusivity

Intersectional approaches to feminism and LGBTQ+ activism recognize the interconnectedness of gender, race, class, sexuality, and other identities.
Advocates work towards creating inclusive spaces that address the unique challenges faced by individuals with intersecting identities.
Conclusion
The history of feminism and the ongoing struggle for gender equality intersect with the fight for LGBTQ+ rights, highlighting the interconnectedness of social justice movements. By understanding the historical context of feminism and the contemporary issues surrounding gender identity and LGBTQ+ rights, societies can work towards creating more inclusive and equitable communities for all individuals, regardless of their gender or sexual orientation. This chapter emphasizes the importance of solidarity, intersectionality, and ongoing advocacy in advancing gender justice and LGBTQ+ rights in the modern world.

Chapter 28: Intersectionality and Its Significance: Case Studies of Prominent Gender Rights Movements

Introduction

Intersectionality, a concept coined by Kimberlé Crenshaw, highlights the interconnected nature of social identities such as race, class, gender, sexuality, and ability, and how they intersect to shape individuals' experiences of privilege and oppression. This chapter explores the significance of intersectionality and examines case studies of prominent gender rights movements that have embraced intersectional approaches to advocacy.

1. Understanding Intersectionality
*1. Intersectionality as a Concept

Intersectionality acknowledges that individuals hold multiple social identities that intersect and interact to shape their experiences of power and privilege.
The concept emphasizes the need to consider the unique and intersecting forms of discrimination and marginalization faced by individuals with multiple marginalized identities.
**2. Significance of Intersectionality

Intersectionality highlights the limitations of single-axis approaches to social justice advocacy and calls for an inclusive and holistic understanding of oppression and inequality.
By centering the experiences of marginalized individuals and communities, intersectional approaches aim to address the root causes of systemic injustices and promote more equitable outcomes for all.
2. Case Studies of Prominent Gender Rights Movements
*1. #MeToo Movement

The #MeToo movement, founded by Tarana Burke and popularized on social media in 2017, raised awareness of sexual harassment and assault experienced by women and marginalized genders.

The movement highlighted the intersectional nature of gender-based violence, recognizing that individuals from diverse backgrounds face unique barriers to seeking justice and support.
**2. Black Lives Matter (BLM) Movement

The Black Lives Matter movement, founded by Alicia Garza, Patrisse Cullors, and Opal Tometi in 2013, advocates for racial justice and an end to police brutality and systemic racism. BLM adopts an intersectional approach, recognizing the ways in which racism intersects with other forms of oppression, including sexism, homophobia, and transphobia, to impact Black communities.
**3. Transgender Rights Advocacy

Transgender rights advocacy movements, such as the Stonewall riots of 1969 and the ongoing fight for transgender equality, highlight the intersectional experiences of transgender and gender-nonconforming individuals. These movements emphasize the importance of centering transgender voices and experiences in the fight for LGBTQ+ rights and social justice.
Conclusion
Intersectionality offers a critical framework for understanding the complex interplay of social identities and power dynamics that shape individuals' lives. By examining case studies of prominent gender rights movements that embrace intersectional approaches, we gain insights into the significance of centering marginalized voices and experiences in advocacy efforts. This chapter underscores the importance of intersectionality in fostering solidarity, inclusivity, and collective action in the pursuit of gender justice and social equality.

Chapter 29: Populism and Nationalism: Global Trends and Case Studies

Introduction

Populism and nationalism have emerged as influential political ideologies shaping contemporary societies worldwide. This chapter explores the rise of populist movements, the proliferation of nationalist ideologies, and the impact of these trends on societies. Through analysis of recent populist leaders and case studies of populism's consequences in various countries, we gain insight into the complexities of these phenomena.

1. Rise of Populist Movements Globally
*1. Defining Populism

Populism is a political approach that claims to represent the interests of ordinary people against a perceived elite or establishment.
Populist movements often emphasize anti-elitism, nativism, and a direct appeal to the emotions and grievances of the populace.
**2. Global Trends in Populism

Populist movements have gained traction in diverse contexts around the world, fueled by factors such as economic insecurity, cultural anxiety, and dissatisfaction with political institutions.
From Europe to the Americas, populist leaders and parties have capitalized on discontent with globalization, immigration, and perceived cultural change.
2. Nationalist Ideologies and Their Impact on Societies
*1. Nationalism and Identity

Nationalism is an ideology that prioritizes the interests and identity of one's own nation or ethnic group above others.
Nationalist movements often emphasize patriotism, cultural preservation, and sovereignty, while sometimes promoting xenophobia and exclusionary policies.
**2. Impact of Nationalism

Nationalist ideologies can galvanize support for policies that prioritize national interests, border control, and cultural homogeneity.

However, nationalism can also exacerbate social divisions, fuel ethnonationalist conflicts, and strain international relations.

3. Analysis of Recent Populist Leaders

*1. Prominent Populist Leaders

Recent years have seen the rise of populist leaders such as Donald Trump in the United States, Viktor Orbán in Hungary, and Jair Bolsonaro in Brazil.

These leaders employ populist rhetoric, often scapegoating marginalized groups and challenging democratic norms and institutions.

**2. Strategies and Tactics

Populist leaders employ a variety of tactics to maintain power and mobilize support, including media manipulation, polarizing rhetoric, and attacks on political opponents and institutions.

By capitalizing on social divisions and grievances, populist leaders seek to consolidate power and reshape political landscapes in their favor.

4. Case Studies: Consequences of Populism in Various Countries

*1. United States: Trump Presidency

The Trump presidency was characterized by populist rhetoric, nationalist policies, and polarization.

Consequences of Trump's populism included heightened political polarization, erosion of democratic norms, and controversies over immigration and race relations.

**2. Hungary: Viktor Orbán's Rule

Viktor Orbán's government in Hungary has pursued a populist-nationalist agenda, consolidating power and undermining democratic institutions.
Orbán's populist policies have led to concerns about authoritarianism, media censorship, and attacks on civil liberties and minority rights.
**3. Brazil: Jair Bolsonaro's Presidency

Jair Bolsonaro's presidency in Brazil has been marked by populist rhetoric, authoritarian tendencies, and controversial policies.
Bolsonaro's populist-nationalist agenda has raised concerns about environmental protection, indigenous rights, and democratic governance in Brazil.
Conclusion
Populism and nationalism have profound implications for political dynamics, social cohesion, and democratic governance in countries around the world. By examining the rise of populist movements, the proliferation of nationalist ideologies, and the consequences of populism in various countries, we gain a deeper understanding of these complex phenomena and their impact on societies. This chapter underscores the importance of critical analysis, civic engagement, and democratic resilience in addressing the challenges posed by populism and nationalism in the 21st century.

Chapter 30: Healthcare Policy: Systems, Debates, and Case Studies

Introduction
Healthcare policy plays a crucial role in determining access to healthcare services, quality of care, and population health outcomes. This chapter provides an overview of different healthcare systems, explores debates on healthcare reform and public health, analyzes the impact of healthcare policies on populations, and examines case studies of successful healthcare models.

1. Overview of Different Healthcare Systems
*1. Universal Healthcare Systems

Universal healthcare systems provide healthcare coverage to all citizens, typically funded through taxation or mandatory insurance schemes.
Examples include single-payer systems (e.g., Medicare in Canada), social health insurance systems (e.g., Germany), and national health services (e.g., NHS in the United Kingdom).
**2. Private Healthcare Systems

Private healthcare systems rely on private insurance and out-of-pocket payments for healthcare services.
Examples include the healthcare systems in the United States and some developing countries where private providers dominate the healthcare landscape.
**3. Hybrid Healthcare Systems

Hybrid healthcare systems combine elements of both public and private healthcare provision.
Examples include the healthcare systems in France and Australia, where a mix of public and private providers coexist.
2. Debates on Healthcare Reform and Public Health
**1. Access vs. Cost

Debates on healthcare reform often center around balancing access to healthcare services with controlling costs.
Advocates for universal healthcare argue that it ensures equitable access to care, while opponents raise concerns about government intervention and fiscal sustainability.
**2. Quality vs. Efficiency

Healthcare reform efforts also grapple with balancing quality of care with efficiency and cost-effectiveness.
Initiatives such as value-based care and accountable care organizations aim to improve healthcare quality while containing costs through better coordination and outcomes measurement.
3. Impact of Healthcare Policies on Populations
**1. Health Outcomes

Healthcare policies have a direct impact on population health outcomes, including measures such as life expectancy, infant mortality, and disease prevalence.
Countries with comprehensive healthcare coverage and strong primary care systems tend to have better health outcomes and lower healthcare disparities.
**2. Health Equity

Healthcare policies can either exacerbate or mitigate health inequities within populations.
Policies that address social determinants of health, promote preventive care, and ensure access to essential services can contribute to greater health equity.

4. Case Studies: Successful Healthcare Models
*1. Canada: Single-Payer Healthcare

Canada's single-payer healthcare system provides universal coverage to all citizens, funded through taxation.
The system prioritizes access to essential healthcare services, resulting in relatively low administrative costs and equitable health outcomes.
**2. Singapore: Mixed Healthcare System

Singapore's mixed healthcare system combines universal coverage with a strong emphasis on personal responsibility and cost-sharing.
The system achieves high levels of healthcare access and quality while controlling costs through market competition and government regulation.
**3. Netherlands: Social Health Insurance

The Netherlands' social health insurance system combines mandatory insurance with private competition and government regulation.
The system emphasizes consumer choice, quality improvement, and cost containment, resulting in high levels of satisfaction and health outcomes.
Conclusion
Healthcare policy is a multifaceted field that encompasses various healthcare systems, debates, and policy interventions. By understanding the strengths and weaknesses of different healthcare models, analyzing debates on healthcare reform and public health, and examining case studies of successful healthcare models, policymakers and stakeholders can work towards creating more effective and equitable healthcare systems that meet the needs of diverse populations. This chapter underscores the importance of evidence-based policymaking, collaboration across sectors, and a commitment to health equity in shaping the future of healthcare policy.

Chapter 31: Criminal Justice Reform: Systems, Calls, and Case Studies

Introduction
Criminal justice reform addresses the structures and practices within the legal system, focusing on issues such as prison systems, policing methods, and the administration of justice. This chapter examines the current state of prison systems and policing, explores calls for justice system reforms, analyzes the impact of reforms on crime and communities, and examines case studies of transformative justice initiatives.

1. Examination of Prison Systems and Policing
**1. Prison Systems

Prison systems vary widely across jurisdictions, but common issues include overcrowding, harsh sentencing laws, and limited access to rehabilitation programs.
Mass incarceration disproportionately impacts marginalized communities, exacerbating racial and socioeconomic disparities within the criminal justice system.
**2. Policing Methods

Policing methods range from community policing and restorative justice approaches to militarized tactics and aggressive enforcement strategies.
Calls for police reform often focus on accountability, transparency, and demilitarization, as well as addressing systemic issues such as racial profiling and police brutality.

2. Calls for and Examples of Justice System Reforms
**1. Sentencing Reform

Calls for sentencing reform advocate for alternatives to incarceration, such as diversion programs, drug courts, and restorative justice initiatives.
Reforms aim to address disparities in sentencing, reduce recidivism rates, and promote rehabilitation and reintegration for individuals involved in the justice system.
**2. Police Accountability

Calls for police accountability center on measures such as civilian oversight boards, body cameras, and independent investigations of police misconduct.
Reform efforts seek to increase transparency, accountability, and trust between law enforcement agencies and the communities they serve.
3. Impact of Reforms on Crime and Communities
**1. Crime Rates

The impact of justice system reforms on crime rates varies depending on the nature of the reforms and the context in which they are implemented.
Evidence suggests that certain reforms, such as diversion programs and community-based interventions, can lead to reductions in recidivism and crime rates.
**2. Community Trust and Well-being

Justice system reforms can improve community trust in law enforcement and the legal system, leading to increased cooperation, safer neighborhoods, and improved well-being for residents.
Restorative justice initiatives that involve community members in resolving conflicts and addressing harm can strengthen social bonds and promote healing within communities.

4. Case Studies: Transformative Justice Initiatives
**1. Community Policing and Restorative Justice

Initiatives such as community policing and restorative justice
programs prioritize community engagement, conflict
resolution, and accountability over punitive measures.
Examples include the Oakland Ceasefire program, which
combines law enforcement efforts with community-based
interventions to reduce gun violence and address root causes
of crime.
**2. Bail and Pretrial Justice Reform

Bail and pretrial justice reforms aim to reduce reliance on cash
bail, address inequalities in pretrial detention, and promote
fair and effective pretrial practices.
Examples include the Pretrial Justice Institute's efforts to
promote risk-based assessments and alternatives to cash bail
in jurisdictions across the United States.
Conclusion
Criminal justice reform is essential for creating fair, equitable,
and effective systems of justice that prioritize public safety,
rehabilitation, and community well-being. By examining the
current state of prison systems and policing, exploring calls
for justice system reforms, analyzing the impact of reforms on
crime and communities, and examining case studies of
transformative justice initiatives, policymakers and
stakeholders can work towards building more just and
inclusive societies. This chapter underscores the importance of
evidence-based policymaking, community engagement, and a
commitment to human rights and social justice in driving
meaningful change within the criminal justice system.

Chapter 32: Media and Fake News: Influence, Issues, and Case Studies

Introduction

The media plays a pivotal role in shaping public opinion, informing citizens, and holding those in power accountable. However, in an era of widespread misinformation and fake news, the integrity of journalism and the trustworthiness of media sources are increasingly questioned. This chapter examines the role of media in shaping public opinion, explores issues of misinformation and fake news, analyzes the impact of journalism on politics, and presents case studies illustrating media's influence on recent events.

1. Role of Media in Shaping Public Opinion
**1. Information Dissemination

The media serves as a primary source of information, disseminating news, analysis, and commentary on current events and issues.
Different media platforms, including traditional outlets, social media, and online news sources, play a role in shaping public discourse and influencing public opinion.
**2. Agenda Setting

Media outlets have the power to set the agenda by deciding which topics and issues receive attention and coverage.

Through editorial decisions, news framing, and coverage priorities, the media can influence public perceptions and priorities.

2. Issues of Misinformation and Fake News

**1. Misinformation

Misinformation refers to false or misleading information spread unintentionally, often due to errors or lack of verification.

Misinformation can spread rapidly through social media and other online platforms, leading to confusion and mistrust among the public.

**2. Fake News

Fake news, on the other hand, refers to deliberately fabricated or manipulated information designed to deceive and manipulate audiences.

Fake news undermines the credibility of journalism, erodes trust in media sources, and threatens the integrity of democratic discourse.

3. Impact of Journalism on Politics

**1. Watchdog Function

Journalism plays a crucial watchdog role in holding government officials and institutions accountable for their actions.

Investigative reporting, whistleblowing, and freedom of the press are essential for exposing corruption, abuses of power, and human rights violations.

**2. Political Polarization

Media coverage can contribute to political polarization by framing issues in ways that reinforce partisan divides and ideological differences.

Echo chambers and filter bubbles created by algorithmic news feeds can exacerbate polarization and limit exposure to diverse perspectives.

4. Case Studies: Media's Influence on Recent Events

**1. 2020 U.S. Presidential Election

Media coverage of the 2020 U.S. presidential election played a significant role in shaping voter perceptions and influencing electoral outcomes.

Coverage of candidates, campaign events, and policy debates influenced voter attitudes and behavior, highlighting the power of media in electoral politics.

**2. COVID-19 Pandemic

Media coverage of the COVID-19 pandemic influenced public perceptions of the virus, government responses, and public health measures.

Dissemination of accurate information, debunking of myths, and coverage of scientific developments were critical in shaping public understanding and behavior during the crisis.

Conclusion

Media and fake news have profound implications for democracy, public discourse, and civic engagement. By examining the role of media in shaping public opinion, exploring issues of misinformation and fake news, analyzing the impact of journalism on politics, and presenting case studies illustrating media's influence on recent events, we gain insight into the complexities of media's role in society. This chapter underscores the importance of media literacy, critical thinking, and ethical journalism practices in navigating the modern media landscape and preserving the integrity of democratic discourse.

Chapter 33: Cybersecurity and Data Privacy: Threats, Importance, and Case Studies

Introduction
In an increasingly digital world, cybersecurity and data privacy are paramount concerns. From personal information to critical infrastructure, safeguarding data from cyber threats is essential for individuals, businesses, and governments alike. This chapter provides an overview of digital security threats, emphasizes the importance of data privacy in the digital age, discusses policies and measures to protect information, and presents case studies of notable cybersecurity breaches and responses.

1. Overview of Digital Security Threats
*1. Cyber Attacks

Cyber attacks encompass a wide range of threats, including malware, phishing, ransomware, and denial-of-service (DoS) attacks.
These attacks target computer systems, networks, and data, seeking to compromise confidentiality, integrity, and availability.
**2. Emerging Threats

Emerging threats such as artificial intelligence (AI) and the Internet of Things (IoT) introduce new vulnerabilities and attack vectors.
AI-powered attacks and IoT botnets pose significant challenges for cybersecurity professionals, requiring adaptive defenses and proactive risk management.
2. Importance of Data Privacy in the Digital Age
**1. Personal Privacy

Data privacy is essential for protecting individuals' personal information from unauthorized access, use, and disclosure. Privacy regulations such as the General Data Protection Regulation (GDPR) and the California Consumer Privacy Act (CCPA) aim to empower individuals with control over their personal data.
**2. Business Trust

Data privacy is crucial for building trust with customers and stakeholders, as breaches can damage reputations and lead to financial losses.
Businesses must prioritize data protection measures and compliance with privacy regulations to maintain trust and credibility.
3. Policies and Measures to Protect Information
**1. Cybersecurity Frameworks

Cybersecurity frameworks provide guidelines and best practices for securing digital assets and mitigating cyber risks. Frameworks such as the NIST Cybersecurity Framework and ISO/IEC 27001 offer structured approaches to risk management and cybersecurity governance.
**2. Encryption and Access Controls

Encryption and access controls are fundamental measures for protecting data both at rest and in transit.

Strong encryption algorithms and robust access controls help prevent unauthorized access and data breaches.
4. Case Studies: Notable Cybersecurity Breaches and Responses
**1. Equifax Data Breach (2017)

The Equifax data breach exposed sensitive personal information of over 147 million consumers, including Social Security numbers and credit card data.
The breach led to congressional hearings, regulatory scrutiny, and a $700 million settlement with the Federal Trade Commission (FTC).
**2. WannaCry Ransomware Attack (2017)

The WannaCry ransomware attack targeted hundreds of thousands of computers worldwide, encrypting data and demanding ransom payments in Bitcoin.
The attack disrupted critical infrastructure, including healthcare systems and transportation networks, highlighting the global impact of cyber threats.
Conclusion
Cybersecurity and data privacy are fundamental aspects of modern digital life, requiring proactive measures and continuous vigilance to protect against evolving threats. By understanding digital security threats, emphasizing the importance of data privacy, implementing policies and measures to protect information, and learning from case studies of cybersecurity breaches and responses, individuals and organizations can strengthen their defenses and mitigate risks in an increasingly interconnected world. This chapter underscores the urgency of cybersecurity awareness, collaboration, and innovation in safeguarding digital assets and preserving trust in the digital age.

Chapter 34: International Relations: Strategies, Conflicts, and Diplomacy

Introduction
International relations shape the dynamics between nations, influencing global stability, cooperation, and conflict resolution. This chapter delves into geopolitical strategies, current international conflicts, the role of international organizations, and case studies of effective diplomatic interventions, highlighting the complexities and significance of international relations in the contemporary world.

1. Geopolitical Strategies and Global Diplomacy
*1. Geopolitical Competition

Geopolitical strategies involve the pursuit of national interests, power projection, and influence in the international arena.
Major powers engage in geopolitical competition through diplomatic, economic, and military means to secure strategic advantages and assert dominance.
**2. Global Diplomacy

Global diplomacy encompasses negotiations, treaties, and diplomatic engagements aimed at resolving conflicts, fostering cooperation, and promoting stability.
Diplomatic efforts involve multilateral forums, bilateral negotiations, and track-two diplomacy initiatives to address global challenges and advance common interests.
2. Current International Conflicts and Resolutions
*1. Regional Conflicts

Regional conflicts, such as those in the Middle East, Ukraine, and the South China Sea, pose challenges to international peace and security.
Efforts to resolve these conflicts often involve diplomatic mediation, peacekeeping operations, and international sanctions to de-escalate tensions and promote dialogue.
**2. Global Challenges

Global challenges, including climate change, terrorism, and pandemics, require international cooperation and collective action to address effectively.
Multilateral initiatives and agreements, such as the Paris Agreement on climate change and the United Nations Security Council resolutions on counterterrorism, aim to mobilize global efforts to tackle shared challenges.
3. Role of International Organizations
*1. United Nations (UN)

The United Nations serves as a central forum for international cooperation, peacekeeping, and conflict resolution.
UN agencies and specialized bodies address a wide range of issues, from humanitarian assistance and development to human rights and disarmament.
**2. Regional Organizations

Regional organizations, such as the European Union, African Union, and Association of Southeast Asian Nations (ASEAN), play pivotal roles in promoting regional stability, economic integration, and conflict resolution.

These organizations facilitate dialogue, cooperation, and mutual assistance among member states to address regional challenges and enhance collective security.

4. Case Studies: Effective Diplomatic Interventions

*1. Iran Nuclear Deal (Joint Comprehensive Plan of Action)

The Iran Nuclear Deal, negotiated in 2015 between Iran and six world powers (P5+1), aimed to limit Iran's nuclear program in exchange for sanctions relief.

The agreement demonstrated the effectiveness of multilateral diplomacy in addressing nuclear proliferation concerns and averting a potential military confrontation.

**2. Normalization of Relations between Israel and Arab States

Recent diplomatic breakthroughs between Israel and several Arab states, including the United Arab Emirates, Bahrain, and Sudan, marked a significant shift in regional dynamics.

Diplomatic efforts, facilitated by regional and international actors, paved the way for normalization agreements that promote stability and cooperation in the Middle East.

Conclusion

International relations play a crucial role in shaping the global order, influencing peace, stability, and cooperation among nations. By understanding geopolitical strategies, current international conflicts, the role of international organizations, and case studies of effective diplomatic interventions, policymakers and stakeholders can navigate complex international challenges and promote a more peaceful and prosperous world. This chapter underscores the importance of diplomacy, dialogue, and multilateral cooperation in addressing global issues and advancing common interests on the international stage.

Chapter 35: Election Integrity and Voting Rights: Challenges, Security, and Case Studies

Introduction
Election integrity and voting rights are fundamental pillars of democracy, ensuring fair and transparent electoral processes that reflect the will of the people. This chapter examines voting rights issues, voter suppression tactics, the importance of election security, strategies to safeguard democratic processes, and case studies of recent elections and integrity challenges.

1. Examination of Voting Rights Issues and Voter Suppression
*1. Voting Rights Legislation

Voting rights legislation shapes who can vote, how they can vote, and under what conditions.
Issues such as voter ID laws, voter registration requirements, and gerrymandering disproportionately affect marginalized communities and can suppress voter turnout.
**2. Voter Suppression Tactics

Voter suppression tactics include voter purges, restrictive voting laws, intimidation tactics, and misinformation campaigns.
These tactics undermine the principles of democracy by disenfranchising eligible voters and undermining public trust in the electoral process.
2. Importance of Election Security
*1. Cybersecurity Threats

Election security is essential for protecting the integrity of elections against cyber threats, foreign interference, and misinformation.
Cyber attacks targeting election infrastructure, voter databases, and electoral systems pose significant risks to the democratic process and public confidence in elections.
**2. Trust in Democratic Processes

Confidence in election security is crucial for ensuring public trust in democratic processes and the legitimacy of election outcomes.
Transparent, auditable, and verifiable election procedures are essential for addressing concerns about fraud and safeguarding the integrity of elections.
3. Strategies to Ensure Democratic Processes
*1. Voter Education and Outreach

Voter education and outreach efforts aim to inform voters about their rights, registration procedures, and voting options.
Civic engagement initiatives, voter registration drives, and community outreach programs help empower citizens to participate in the democratic process.
**2. Legal Protections and Advocacy

Legal protections and advocacy efforts seek to defend voting rights, challenge voter suppression tactics, and promote inclusive electoral practices.
Civil rights organizations, advocacy groups, and legal experts play critical roles in litigating voting rights cases and advancing electoral reforms.
4. Case Studies: Recent Elections and Integrity Challenges
*1. United States: 2020 Presidential Election

The 2020 U.S. presidential election saw unprecedented voter turnout and heightened concerns about election security and integrity.
Despite baseless claims of widespread fraud, election officials, cybersecurity experts, and independent audits affirmed the integrity and accuracy of the election results.
**2. Kenya: 2017 Presidential Election

The 2017 Kenyan presidential election was marred by allegations of electoral fraud, irregularities, and violence.
The Supreme Court of Kenya nullified the election results due to irregularities, highlighting the importance of independent oversight and judicial review in safeguarding electoral integrity.
Conclusion
Election integrity and voting rights are cornerstones of democracy, requiring vigilance, advocacy, and concerted efforts to protect and preserve. By examining voting rights issues, voter suppression tactics, the importance of election security, strategies to ensure democratic processes, and case studies of recent elections and integrity challenges, we gain insights into the complexities and significance of electoral integrity in democratic societies. This chapter underscores the importance of safeguarding voting rights, strengthening election security measures, and upholding the principles of democracy to ensure free, fair, and credible elections for all citizens.

Chapter 36: Mental Health in Society: Intersection, Impact, and Initiatives

Introduction
Mental health is an integral component of overall well-being, influencing individual resilience, community cohesion, and societal prosperity. This chapter explores the intersection of mental health and social issues, the impact of mental health on communities, policies and programs for mental health support, and case studies of innovative mental health initiatives.

1. Intersection of Mental Health and Social Issues
*1. Social Determinants of Mental Health

Social determinants such as poverty, discrimination, trauma, and social isolation profoundly impact mental health outcomes.

Addressing social inequalities and systemic barriers is essential for promoting mental health equity and reducing disparities.
**2. Stigma and Discrimination

Stigma and discrimination surrounding mental illness contribute to social exclusion, barriers to treatment, and negative health outcomes.
Anti-stigma campaigns, education initiatives, and community-based interventions aim to challenge stigma and promote understanding and acceptance.
2. Impact of Mental Health on Communities
*1. Public Health Burden

Mental health disorders represent a significant public health burden, affecting individuals, families, and communities.
The economic costs of untreated mental illness, including healthcare expenses, lost productivity, and reduced quality of life, underscore the importance of early intervention and prevention efforts.
**2. Community Resilience

Strong social support networks, community resources, and resilience-building programs can enhance community resilience and mitigate the impact of mental health challenges.
Community-based mental health services, peer support groups, and crisis intervention programs offer vital resources for individuals facing mental health crises.
3. Policies and Programs for Mental Health Support
*1. Mental Health Policy Frameworks

Mental health policy frameworks provide guidelines and strategies for promoting mental health, preventing mental illness, and ensuring access to quality care.

Comprehensive mental health policies encompass prevention, early intervention, treatment, and recovery support across the lifespan.
**2. Integrated Care Models

Integrated care models, such as collaborative care and co-located services, integrate mental health services with primary care and community-based supports.
These models improve access to mental health care, reduce stigma, and address the complex needs of individuals with mental health conditions.
4. Case Studies: Innovative Mental Health Initiatives
*1. The Friendship Bench (Zimbabwe)

The Friendship Bench program in Zimbabwe employs lay health workers to provide evidence-based psychological interventions, including problem-solving therapy and cognitive-behavioral techniques.
The program has demonstrated success in improving mental health outcomes and community resilience, particularly in underserved urban areas.
*2. Thrive NYC (New York City)

Thrive NYC is a comprehensive mental health initiative launched by the City of New York to address mental health disparities and improve access to care.
The initiative includes a range of programs and services, such as mental health first aid training, school-based mental health supports, and community outreach efforts.
Conclusion

Mental health is a critical component of individual well-being and societal flourishing, requiring collective action and commitment to promote mental health equity and support those in need. By exploring the intersection of mental health and social issues, understanding the impact of mental health on communities, examining policies and programs for mental health support, and highlighting case studies of innovative mental health initiatives, we gain insight into effective strategies for addressing mental health challenges in society. This chapter underscores the importance of fostering resilience, reducing stigma, and building inclusive, supportive communities that prioritize mental health and well-being for all.

Chapter 37: Education Policy: Systems, Equality, and Reforms

Introduction
Education policy plays a pivotal role in shaping the quality, accessibility, and equity of educational opportunities for individuals and communities. This chapter provides an analysis of current education systems and reforms, examines issues of access and equality in education, explores the impact of policies on educational outcomes, and presents case studies of successful education reforms.

1. Analysis of Current Education Systems and Reforms

*1. Education System Structures

Education systems vary globally in terms of structure, governance, and funding mechanisms.
Common features include public and private school options, standardized testing, and curriculum frameworks tailored to national or regional contexts.
**2. Reform Efforts

Education reforms aim to improve teaching and learning outcomes, enhance educational access and equity, and respond to changing societal needs.
Reforms may focus on curriculum revisions, teacher training programs, assessment methods, or school governance structures.
2. Access to Education and Equality Issues
*1. Educational Equity

Educational equity encompasses ensuring that all students have access to resources, opportunities, and support systems needed to succeed academically.
Equity issues may include disparities in funding, access to quality teachers, school facilities, and educational materials.
**2. Barriers to Access

Barriers to educational access may include socioeconomic factors, geographic location, cultural barriers, language proficiency, and disabilities.
Efforts to address access barriers may involve targeted interventions such as scholarships, transportation assistance, and community outreach programs.
3. Impact of Policies on Educational Outcomes
*1. Policy Interventions

Education policies can have a significant impact on student achievement, graduation rates, and workforce readiness.

Effective policies may include class size reduction initiatives, early childhood education programs, and college affordability measures.

**2. Assessment and Accountability

Assessment and accountability measures, such as standardized testing and school accountability systems, shape teaching practices and educational priorities.
Criticisms of high-stakes testing include concerns about narrowing curriculum focus, teaching to the test, and exacerbating inequities.
4. Case Studies: Successful Education Reforms
*1. Finland's Education System

Finland's education system is internationally renowned for its emphasis on equity, teacher professionalism, and student well-being.
Key features include a strong emphasis on teacher training, school autonomy, and a holistic, student-centered approach to learning.
*2. Singapore's Education Reforms

Singapore's education reforms have focused on promoting excellence, meritocracy, and lifelong learning.
Initiatives such as the "Teach Less, Learn More" pedagogical approach and SkillsFuture program aim to prepare students for the challenges of the future economy.
Conclusion

Education policy plays a vital role in shaping the quality, accessibility, and equity of educational opportunities for individuals and communities. By analyzing current education systems and reforms, examining issues of access and equality, exploring the impact of policies on educational outcomes, and presenting case studies of successful education reforms, we gain insight into effective strategies for improving educational outcomes and promoting equity in education. This chapter underscores the importance of evidence-based policymaking, collaboration among stakeholders, and a commitment to inclusive, student-centered approaches to education reform.

Chapter 38: Urban Development and Housing: Challenges, Gentrification, and Solutions

Introduction

Urban development and housing are critical components of sustainable urbanization, affecting the quality of life, economic opportunities, and social cohesion within cities. This chapter addresses issues of affordable housing, urban planning, the impact of gentrification on communities, policies for sustainable urban development, and case studies of effective urban development projects.

1. Issues of Affordable Housing and Urban Planning
*1. Housing Affordability Crisis

Many cities face a housing affordability crisis, with skyrocketing housing costs outpacing income growth. Factors contributing to the crisis include limited housing supply, rising land prices, and inadequate affordable housing policies.
**2. Urban Planning Challenges

Urban planning plays a crucial role in shaping the built environment, infrastructure, and land use within cities. Challenges include balancing competing interests, addressing community needs, and promoting equitable development outcomes.
2. Impact of Gentrification on Communities
*1. Gentrification Dynamics

Gentrification refers to the process of urban renewal and revitalization, often accompanied by displacement of lower-income residents.
Gentrification can lead to increased property values, changes in neighborhood demographics, and cultural shifts within communities.
**2. Displacement and Social Equity

Gentrification can exacerbate social inequalities and displacement pressures, particularly for marginalized communities.
Strategies to mitigate displacement may include affordable housing mandates, tenant protections, and community land trusts.
3. Policies for Sustainable Urban Development
*1. Affordable Housing Strategies

Affordable housing policies aim to increase housing affordability through subsidies, rent control, inclusionary zoning, and public-private partnerships.
Mixed-income housing developments and community land trusts promote diverse and inclusive neighborhoods.
**2. Smart Growth and Transit-Oriented Development

Smart growth principles emphasize compact, mixed-use development, walkable neighborhoods, and access to public transit.
Transit-oriented development (TOD) focuses on creating vibrant, connected communities around transit nodes, reducing car dependency and promoting sustainable mobility.
4. Case Studies: Effective Urban Development Projects
*1. Vauban, Freiburg (Germany)

Vauban is a sustainable urban development project in Freiburg, Germany, known for its car-free streets, energy-efficient buildings, and community participation.
The neighborhood prioritizes environmental sustainability, social inclusion, and participatory decision-making processes.
*2. Medellín (Colombia) Urban Transformation

Medellín's urban transformation initiatives have revitalized former slums and marginalized areas through investments in public transportation, infrastructure, and social programs.

Projects such as the Metrocable system and cultural centers have improved mobility, connectivity, and social inclusion in underserved neighborhoods.

Conclusion

Urban development and housing present complex challenges and opportunities for cities striving to create equitable, sustainable, and inclusive communities. By addressing issues of affordable housing, urban planning, the impact of gentrification, policies for sustainable urban development, and case studies of effective urban development projects, cities can foster vibrant, resilient, and livable environments for all residents. This chapter underscores the importance of holistic, people-centered approaches to urban development that prioritize social equity, environmental sustainability, and community participation.

Chapter 39: Civil Liberties and Human Rights: Freedom, Challenges, and Victories

Introduction
Civil liberties and human rights are fundamental principles that underpin democratic societies, safeguarding individual freedoms, dignity, and equality. This chapter examines freedom of speech, privacy rights, and civil liberties, explores challenges to human rights in modern societies, discusses the role of international bodies in protecting rights, and presents case studies of key human rights victories.

1. Examination of Freedom of Speech, Privacy Rights, and Civil Liberties
*1. Freedom of Speech

Freedom of speech is a cornerstone of democracy, allowing individuals to express their opinions, ideas, and beliefs without censorship or restraint.
Challenges to freedom of speech include censorship, hate speech, online harassment, and restrictions on political dissent.
**2. Privacy Rights and Civil Liberties

Privacy rights protect individuals' autonomy, dignity, and personal information from unwarranted intrusion and surveillance.
Civil liberties encompass a range of rights and freedoms, including the right to privacy, freedom of assembly, and due process under the law.
2. Challenges to Human Rights in Modern Societies

*1. Emerging Threats

Human rights face challenges from emerging threats such as authoritarianism, populism, terrorism, and digital surveillance.
These threats undermine democratic values, erode rule of law, and restrict individual freedoms in the name of national security or public safety.
**2. Vulnerable Populations

Vulnerable populations, including refugees, migrants, minorities, and marginalized communities, face heightened risks of discrimination, violence, and human rights abuses.
Addressing systemic inequalities and structural barriers is essential for ensuring the protection of rights for all individuals.
3. Role of International Bodies in Protecting Rights
*1. United Nations (UN)

The United Nations plays a central role in promoting and protecting human rights through treaties, conventions, and international mechanisms.
Specialized UN agencies, such as the Office of the High Commissioner for Human Rights (OHCHR), monitor human rights situations, provide technical assistance, and support advocacy efforts.
**2. Regional Human Rights Bodies

Regional human rights bodies, such as the European Court of Human Rights and the Inter-American Commission on Human Rights, complement the work of the UN by adjudicating human rights cases and monitoring compliance with regional treaties.
These bodies offer avenues for redress and accountability at the regional level, complementing national human rights institutions and domestic legal systems.

4. Case Studies: Key Human Rights Victories
*1. Marriage Equality

The legalization of same-sex marriage in numerous countries represents a significant victory for LGBTQ+ rights and marriage equality.
Landmark cases and legislative reforms have affirmed the right to marry and the principle of non-discrimination based on sexual orientation or gender identity.
**2. Reproductive Rights

Advances in reproductive rights, including access to contraception, abortion services, and reproductive healthcare, have expanded reproductive autonomy and gender equality. Legal victories and advocacy efforts have challenged restrictive laws, expanded access to reproductive services, and affirmed reproductive rights as fundamental human rights.
Conclusion
Civil liberties and human rights are essential safeguards against oppression, discrimination, and injustice, protecting the dignity and autonomy of individuals worldwide. By examining freedom of speech, privacy rights, challenges to human rights, the role of international bodies, and case studies of key human rights victories, we gain insight into the complexities and significance of human rights in contemporary societies. This chapter underscores the importance of upholding human rights principles, defending vulnerable populations, and promoting justice, equality, and dignity for all individuals, regardless of race, gender, religion, or identity.

Chapter 40: Technology and Society: Impacts, Ethics, and Innovations

Introduction
Technology has become an integral part of modern society, shaping how we live, work, communicate, and interact with the world around us. This chapter explores the impact of technological advancements on society, ethical considerations and policy implications, the balance between innovation and societal needs, and case studies illustrating technology's role in societal change.

1. Impact of Technological Advancements on Society
*1. Digital Transformation

Technological advancements, such as artificial intelligence, automation, and the Internet of Things, are driving a digital transformation across industries and sectors.
These technologies have the potential to enhance productivity, improve efficiency, and enable new forms of communication and collaboration.
**2. Social and Cultural Changes

Technology has reshaped social dynamics, cultural norms, and patterns of behavior, influencing how we connect, consume information, and express ourselves.
Social media platforms, online communities, and digital entertainment have transformed how we socialize, entertain, and engage with the world.

2. Ethical Considerations and Policy Implications
*1. Privacy and Data Protection

Ethical considerations surrounding technology include issues of privacy, data protection, and surveillance.
Policies such as the General Data Protection Regulation (GDPR) aim to safeguard individuals' privacy rights and regulate the collection and use of personal data.
**2. Algorithmic Bias and Discrimination

Ethical concerns arise from algorithmic bias, where automated systems perpetuate or amplify existing biases and discrimination.
Policy responses may include algorithmic transparency, fairness assessments, and bias mitigation strategies to ensure equitable outcomes.
3. Balancing Innovation with Societal Needs
*1. Technological Innovation

Technological innovation drives economic growth, fosters creativity, and addresses societal challenges through new solutions and advancements.
Policies that support research and development, entrepreneurship, and digital literacy can foster a culture of innovation and entrepreneurship.
**2. Societal Impacts and Equity

Balancing innovation with societal needs requires considering the broader impacts of technological change on individuals, communities, and the environment.
Policies promoting inclusive innovation, equitable access to technology, and responsible technology development can address disparities and promote social justice.
4. Case Studies: Technology's Role in Societal Change
*1. Smart Cities Initiatives

Smart cities initiatives leverage technology to improve urban infrastructure, transportation systems, and public services.
Case studies such as Barcelona's smart city projects demonstrate how technology can enhance sustainability, efficiency, and quality of life for urban residents.
*2. Digital Healthcare Innovations

Digital healthcare innovations, such as telemedicine, wearable devices, and health tracking apps, are transforming healthcare delivery and patient outcomes.
Case studies of digital health initiatives highlight how technology can improve access to healthcare, empower patients, and enhance preventive care.
Conclusion
Technology plays a transformative role in shaping society, with far-reaching implications for individuals, communities, and institutions. By exploring the impact of technological advancements, ethical considerations and policy implications, the balance between innovation and societal needs, and case studies of technology's role in societal change, we gain insight into the complex interplay between technology and society. This chapter underscores the importance of ethical technology development, inclusive innovation practices, and responsive policy frameworks that prioritize human values, societal well-being, and sustainability in the digital age.

Chapter 41: Drug Policy and Substance Abuse: Laws, Treatment, and Reform

Introduction
Drug policy and substance abuse are complex issues with significant social, health, and legal implications. This chapter provides an analysis of current drug laws and their impacts, explores approaches to addiction treatment and prevention, and examines debates on drug policy reform.

1. Analysis of Current Drug Laws and Their Impacts
*1. Drug Classification Systems

Drug laws categorize substances based on their perceived risks and potential for abuse, often leading to disparities in enforcement and sentencing.
The classification of drugs as legal, illegal, or controlled substances varies across jurisdictions and can impact access to treatment, criminalization, and public health outcomes.
**2. Impact on Communities

Drug laws and enforcement policies can disproportionately affect marginalized communities, contributing to racial disparities in arrests, incarceration rates, and access to healthcare.
The criminalization of drug use can perpetuate cycles of poverty, stigmatization, and social exclusion, exacerbating substance abuse issues.
2. Approaches to Addiction Treatment and Prevention

*1. Harm Reduction Strategies

Harm reduction approaches prioritize reducing the negative consequences of drug use, such as overdose deaths and transmission of infectious diseases.
Strategies may include needle exchange programs, supervised injection sites, and opioid agonist therapy to mitigate risks associated with substance abuse.
**2. Evidence-Based Treatment

Evidence-based treatment approaches, such as medication-assisted therapy (MAT), cognitive-behavioral therapy (CBT), and support groups, aim to address the underlying causes of addiction and support recovery.
Access to comprehensive treatment services, including detoxification, counseling, and social support, is essential for addressing substance abuse disorders effectively.
3. Debates on Drug Policy Reform
*1. Decriminalization vs. Legalization

Debates on drug policy reform often center on decriminalization, legalization, and regulation of illicit substances.
Decriminalization involves removing criminal penalties for personal drug use, while legalization entails regulated access to drugs for recreational or medicinal purposes.
**2. Public Health vs. Criminal Justice Approach

Proponents of drug policy reform argue for shifting from a criminal justice approach to a public health approach to substance abuse.
Emphasizing prevention, harm reduction, and treatment over punitive measures can reduce the social and health consequences of drug use while respecting individuals' rights and dignity.
Conclusion

Drug policy and substance abuse are multifaceted issues that require comprehensive, evidence-based approaches grounded in principles of public health, social justice, and human rights. By analyzing current drug laws and their impacts, exploring approaches to addiction treatment and prevention, and examining debates on drug policy reform, we gain insight into the complexities of addressing substance abuse in society. This chapter underscores the importance of adopting compassionate, pragmatic approaches to drug policy that prioritize harm reduction, treatment, and support for individuals struggling with substance abuse disorders.

Chapter 42: Case Studies: Effective Substance Abuse Programs

Introduction
Effective substance abuse programs play a crucial role in addressing addiction, supporting recovery, and reducing the harm associated with substance abuse. This chapter presents case studies of successful programs that have made significant strides in combating substance abuse and improving outcomes for individuals and communities.

1. The Phoenix Multisport Program (United States)
Overview:
The Phoenix Multisport Program is a nonprofit organization that harnesses the power of physical activity and community support to help individuals in recovery from substance abuse and addiction.

Approach:

The program offers a wide range of fitness activities, including rock climbing, yoga, hiking, and strength training, providing participants with opportunities for physical activity and social connection.
Participants engage in activities alongside peers who understand their struggles, fostering a sense of belonging, accountability, and support.
Impact:

The Phoenix Multisport Program has helped thousands of individuals maintain sobriety, improve physical and mental health, and build a supportive community.

Participants report increased self-esteem, reduced cravings, and improved overall well-being as a result of their involvement in the program.

2. Insite Supervised Injection Site (Canada)

Overview:

Insite is a supervised injection site located in Vancouver, Canada, that provides a safe and supportive environment for individuals who use drugs intravenously.

Approach:

Insite offers sterile injection equipment, overdose prevention services, and access to medical care and addiction treatment resources.

Trained staff members provide nonjudgmental support, monitor for signs of overdose, and intervene in emergencies to save lives.

Impact:

Insite has been associated with reductions in overdose deaths, HIV and hepatitis C transmission rates, and public drug use. The site has facilitated access to addiction treatment and other healthcare services, connecting individuals with resources to support their recovery journey.

3. Dianova Therapeutic Community (Costa Rica)

Overview:

Dianova is a therapeutic community in Costa Rica that provides residential treatment and rehabilitation services for individuals struggling with substance abuse and addiction.

Approach:

The therapeutic community model emphasizes peer support, accountability, and holistic recovery approaches.

Participants engage in structured daily activities, including counseling, vocational training, and community building exercises, to address the underlying causes of addiction and develop coping skills for long-term recovery.

Impact:

Dianova has a high success rate in achieving sustained recovery among program participants, with many individuals maintaining sobriety and reintegrating into society as productive, healthy individuals.

The program's emphasis on holistic healing, self-development, and social reintegration has contributed to its effectiveness in addressing substance abuse issues.

Conclusion

Effective substance abuse programs demonstrate the power of compassionate, evidence-based approaches in supporting individuals on their journey to recovery. By highlighting case studies such as the Phoenix Multisport Program, Insite Supervised Injection Site, and Dianova Therapeutic Community, we gain insight into the diverse strategies and interventions that can make a meaningful difference in addressing substance abuse and improving outcomes for individuals and communities. This chapter underscores the importance of investing in innovative, community-driven solutions that prioritize harm reduction, treatment, and support for individuals affected by substance abuse disorders.

Conclusion:

Throughout this exploration of various topics within politics, social sciences, and societal issues, several key themes and insights have emerged:

Complexity and Interconnectedness: The challenges facing society, whether in politics, social justice, or healthcare, are often multifaceted and interconnected. Solutions require a nuanced understanding of the underlying issues and their interdependencies.

Equity and Inclusion: Across different domains, the importance of equity and inclusion has been evident. Whether discussing racial justice, economic inequality, or healthcare access, addressing disparities and ensuring that all individuals have equal opportunities and rights is paramount.

Impact of Technology: Technological advancements have transformed societies in profound ways, influencing how we communicate, work, and interact. However, these advancements also raise ethical considerations, such as privacy rights and algorithmic bias, that require careful attention and regulation.

Human Rights and Social Justice: Discussions on civil liberties, human rights, and social justice highlight the ongoing struggle for equality and dignity. From addressing systemic racism to advocating for LGBTQ+ rights, protecting fundamental freedoms and promoting justice remains a constant endeavor.

Innovative Solutions: Despite the challenges, there are numerous examples of innovative solutions and successful initiatives addressing societal issues. Whether through community-based programs, policy reforms, or grassroots movements, collective action can drive positive change.

Holistic Approaches: Effective solutions often require holistic approaches that consider not only the immediate problem but also its root causes and broader societal impacts. Integrating perspectives from various disciplines and stakeholders can lead to more sustainable and inclusive outcomes.

In conclusion, navigating the complexities of today's world requires a commitment to understanding, empathy, and collaboration. By addressing systemic injustices, promoting equity and inclusion, harnessing the potential of technology responsibly, and embracing innovative solutions, we can work towards building a more just, equitable, and sustainable society for all.

The interconnectedness of politics and social issues is undeniable, as each profoundly influences the other in a continuous cycle of impact and response. Here's how this interconnectedness manifests:

Policy Decisions and Social Impacts: Political decisions, whether made by governments or other governing bodies, directly affect social conditions and outcomes. For instance, changes in healthcare policy can impact access to healthcare services, affecting the well-being of individuals and communities.

Social Movements and Political Change: Social movements, such as civil rights movements or environmental activism, often drive political change by raising awareness, mobilizing public support, and pressuring policymakers to enact reforms. Political leaders, in turn, respond to societal demands and pressures by shaping policies and legislation.

Representation and Advocacy: Politics plays a crucial role in representing diverse social interests and advocating for marginalized communities. Elected officials and political parties may champion specific social issues, such as gender equality or immigration reform, shaping the political agenda and policy priorities.

Power Dynamics and Social Inequality: Political structures and systems can perpetuate or challenge social inequalities and power dynamics. For example, policies related to taxation, education, or criminal justice can either exacerbate disparities or promote equity and justice within society.

Public Discourse and Social Norms: Political discourse and rhetoric shape societal norms, attitudes, and values. Debates around issues like human rights, identity politics, or economic policies influence public perceptions and behaviors, contributing to broader social changes.

Globalization and Transnational Issues: Politics and social issues are increasingly interconnected on a global scale due to processes like globalization. Global political decisions, such as trade agreements or climate accords, have far-reaching social implications that transcend national borders.

Understanding and addressing the interconnectedness of politics and social issues requires recognizing the complex interplay between governance, societal dynamics, and human experiences. By fostering dialogue, collaboration, and inclusive decision-making processes, societies can navigate these interconnected challenges more effectively and work towards positive social change.

As we delve into the intricate web of politics and social issues, it becomes abundantly clear that change is not a passive process but an active endeavor that requires the collective efforts of individuals like you. Here's a call to action to inspire readers to engage and contribute to positive change:

Educate Yourself: Knowledge is power. Take the time to educate yourself on the pressing political and social issues facing your community and the world. Seek out diverse perspectives, reliable sources, and factual information to form well-informed opinions.

Amplify Marginalized Voices: Use your platform, whether it's on social media, in your workplace, or within your community, to amplify the voices of marginalized groups and advocate for their rights and concerns. Actively listen to their experiences, stories, and struggles, and use your privilege to advocate for justice and equality.

Get Involved: Take action by getting involved in local organizations, community groups, or grassroots movements that are working towards positive change. Whether it's volunteering your time, attending rallies and protests, or participating in advocacy campaigns, your involvement can make a tangible difference.

Vote and Advocate: Exercise your civic duty by participating in the political process. Register to vote, stay informed about candidates and issues, and cast your ballot in elections. Additionally, advocate for policies and candidates that align with your values and prioritize social justice, human rights, and environmental sustainability.

Support and Empower Others: Support initiatives and organizations that are working to address systemic inequalities and empower marginalized communities. Donate your resources, time, or skills to causes that resonate with you, and encourage others to do the same.

Challenge Injustice: Speak out against injustice and discrimination wherever you encounter it. Challenge biased attitudes, discriminatory policies, and harmful stereotypes, and work to create inclusive spaces where everyone feels valued and respected.

Commit to Continuous Learning and Growth: Recognize that change is an ongoing process that requires continuous learning, reflection, and growth. Stay open-minded, humble, and receptive to feedback, and be willing to reevaluate your beliefs and actions as you strive to be a more effective agent of change.

By heeding this call to action and taking meaningful steps to engage and contribute to positive change, you can play a vital role in shaping a more just, equitable, and inclusive society for all. Together, let's build a future where every individual's rights, dignity, and well-being are respected and protected.

Below is a glossary of key terms used throughout the book:

Systemic Racism: Structural discrimination or bias embedded within societal institutions and systems, resulting in unequal treatment and outcomes for marginalized racial groups.

Environmental Activism: Advocacy and action aimed at protecting the natural environment, addressing environmental degradation, and promoting sustainability.

Refugee Crisis: A situation characterized by a large influx of forcibly displaced individuals seeking refuge from conflict, persecution, or environmental disasters.

Political Polarization: The divergence of political attitudes and ideologies to extremes, leading to increased ideological division and gridlock within society.

Globalization: The process of increased interconnectedness and interdependence among countries, economies, and cultures through trade, communication, and technological advancements.

Economic Inequality: Disparities in wealth, income, and opportunities within a society, often resulting from structural factors such as unequal access to education, employment, and resources.

Feminism: A social and political movement advocating for gender equality and the empowerment of women in all aspects of society.

Populism: Political ideology or movement that claims to represent the interests of the common people against perceived elites, often characterized by anti-establishment rhetoric and appeals to nationalism.

Healthcare Policy: Government regulations, laws, and programs governing the provision, financing, and delivery of healthcare services to individuals and populations.

Criminal Justice Reform: Efforts to address systemic issues within the criminal justice system, including policing practices, incarceration rates, and sentencing policies, with a focus on fairness, equity, and rehabilitation.

Media Literacy: The ability to critically analyze and evaluate media content, including news, advertisements, and social media, to discern bias, misinformation, and propaganda.

Cybersecurity: Measures and practices aimed at protecting digital systems, networks, and data from cyber threats, including hacking, malware, and data breaches.

International Relations: The study of interactions and relations between nations, including diplomacy, conflict resolution, and international organizations.

Voting Rights: Legal rights and protections ensuring citizens' ability to participate in elections and political decision-making processes without discrimination or barriers.

Mental Health: Emotional, psychological, and social well-being, encompassing mental illness, disorders, and the promotion of mental wellness and resilience.

Urban Development: Planning and management of cities and urban areas, including infrastructure, housing, transportation, and environmental sustainability.

Civil Liberties: Fundamental rights and freedoms guaranteed to individuals by law, such as freedom of speech, religion, and assembly, as well as privacy rights and due process.

Algorithmic Bias: Discriminatory outcomes or decisions resulting from the use of algorithms, often reflecting and perpetuating existing biases and inequalities within society.

Substance Abuse: The harmful or hazardous use of psychoactive substances, including alcohol, drugs, and prescription medications, leading to addiction, dependence, and negative health consequences.

Harm Reduction: Public health approach focused on minimizing the negative consequences associated with substance use, including overdose, infectious diseases, and social harms, through education, prevention, and intervention strategies.

This glossary provides definitions of key terms to aid readers in understanding the concepts discussed throughout the book.